PRAISE FOR

Hope 4 You

Carole Lewis is the living, breathing, flesh-and-blood definition of hope. When she writes a book on this subject, you can count on it. But this is more than just a book to read: it is a book to absorb, to marinate in. *Hope 4 You* is full of gritty and seasoned wisdom and will offer a lifeline if you are drowning in regret and hopelessness. As Carole says, we are "hardwired for hope." This book will act as your technical manual for how to keep hope running and alive.

Jennifer Kennedy Dean

Executive Director of The Praying Life Foundation
Bestselling author of *Live a Praying Life* and numerous books and Bible studies

Carole Lewis is a shining example of the life-changing power of hope—hope that comes from a passionate and personal relationship with Jesus Christ. Her story always inspires me, humbles me, convicts me and challenges me to find my hope in Him, too!

Christin Ditchfield

Author and conference speaker
Host of the syndicated radio program *Take It to Heart!*®

Carole Lewis in one of the most positive women I know. Any woman who has gone through the loss of a child, loss of her home, loss of her parents and who lives with a husband with stage 4 cancer and can still smile and laugh is a woman I want to listen to and go to when I need hope! *Hope 4 You* is better than a cup of cold water on a desert's summer day—or that ray of sunshine in the midst of life's torrential storm. Carole has been there in the middle of the unwelcome, unwanted and unpredictable and has found her way to hope. She will lead you to that precious, hopeful place as well.

Pam Farrel

Relationship specialist, international speaker and author of more than 30 books
Co-director of Farrel Communications and president of Seasoned Sisters

Once again, Carole Lewis has brought us hope in the midst of unexpected and seemingly impossible situations! In *Hope 4 You*, she not only teaches us how to be people of hope through biblical principles and her own amazing story, but she also offers countless testimonies of how God changes lives from the inside out. Read this book for both its practical teaching as well as for inspiration—and then embrace the God of hope for your own life circumstances, because truly, He is there waiting for you.

Lucinda Secrest McDowell
Speaker and author of *God's Purpose for You* and *30 Ways to Embrace Life*

Carole Lewis

with Carolyn Curtis

hope 4 you

God's Plan for Your Health and Happiness

Regal

From Gospel Light
Ventura, California, U.S.A.

Published by Regal
From Gospel Light
Ventura, California, U.S.A.
www.regalbooks.com
Printed in the U.S.A.

Library of Congress Cataloging-in-Publication Data
Lewis, Carole, 1942-
Hope 4 you : God's plan for your health and happiness / Carole Lewis.
p. cm.
ISBN 978-0-8307-5529-5 (hardcover)
1. Spiritual life—Christianity. 2. Hope—Religious aspects—Christianity. I. Title. II. Title: Hope for you. III. Title: God's plan for your health and happiness.
BV4501.3.L4925 2010
248—dc22
2010029912

1 2 3 4 5 6 7 8 9 10 11 12 13 14 15 / 20 19 18 17 16 15 14 13 12 11 10

Rights for publishing this book outside the U.S.A. or in non-English languages are administered by Gospel Light Worldwide, an international not-for-profit ministry. For additional information, please visit www.glww.org, email info@glww.org, or write to Gospel Light Worldwide, 1957 Eastman Avenue, Ventura, CA 93003, U.S.A.

To order copies of this book and other Regal products in bulk quantities, please contact us at 1-800-446-7735.

God has blessed my life with two wonderful women named Lisa: Lisa Cramer, my daughter, and Lisa Lewis, my daughter-in-love. Hope 4 You *is dedicated to both of you with my love and gratitude for all you mean to so many in our First Place 4 Health family and for all you mean to me and our family.*

Contents

INTRODUCTION

My Hope 4 Readers

From everyone who has been given much, much will be demanded; and from the one who has been entrusted with much, much will be asked.
LUKE 12:48

When I was 12, I read Luke 12:48 and knew it was meant for me. I had recently given my life to the Lord, and I'd heard that some children lived in difficult—even abusive—circumstances. I did not; I was well loved and cared for. Life was happy and secure . . . I was "given much." As God filled my heart with hope that my life would continue on this course, I felt drawn to a purpose that this Scripture seemed to capture: Much would be asked of me. Although at that tender age I probably didn't analyze it this carefully, I sensed that I would be able to deliver on whatever God expected.

A few years after my salvation experience, plus discipleship in a nurturing church and family who also made commitments to the Lord, I found the love of my life, Johnny. We would marry when I was still a teen, have three wonderful children and enjoy productive work lives, which for me included ministry.

So far, so good, you may think. *Sounds like the hopes of that 12-year-old new Christian were unfolding pretty much as she expected. She even had ministry work to carry out the part about "giving back."*

And I would agree, not knowing that in a few decades . . .

- My husband and I would declare bankruptcy.
- A drunk driver would kill our precious daughter.
- I would care for the mom I adored as she slipped away.
- Johnny would battle stage IV prostate cancer for years.
- A hurricane would wipe out our home and possessions.

Please don't start comparing me to Job. That would be a very poor comparison, because he was far more righteous and faithful. (I have failed the Lord many times, but He has never failed me.) The comparison of my life to Job's would also be the wrong path, because you would miss the point of this book, which is that *God always provides hope.* Not only is God the source of our hope, but He also teaches us how to build a fortress around our hope. God provides us with resources that we may not even recognize (especially when we feel hopeless), such as our ability to walk personally with Him; how He empowers us to praise Him and be thankful in all circumstances; plus other resources I will describe in this book.

I have written numerous books as national director of First Place 4 Health, a Christ-centered healthy living program that emphasizes balance in the physical, mental, emotional and spiritual areas of life. If you have not read any other book of mine, you may be relieved to learn that I provide encouraging examples from the lives of many other people—not just from my own life! Each chapter in *Hope 4 You* includes stories about people, some written in their own voice, and a few as interviews, all of them providing hope.

Of course, I've included several of the always popular stories about First Place 4 Health leaders and participants that demonstrate how the First Place 4 Health program is helping them lead healthy lives. Like other people's stories—and mine—they include candid descriptions of pain as well as hope.

In the spirit of balance, I will add that my personal bulleted list of joys would be pages and pages long. So please don't think that the five tragedies listed in this introduction define my life, even though they have influenced my growth as a Christian and deepened my walk with my Savior. I will share with you more details about these troubles than I ever have before, but I'll also share how they led me to a place of great and abiding hope.

My hope for you, dear reader, is that God will bless you greatly as you read and reflect.

Carole Lewis
Houston, Texas

1

The Source of Hope

May the God of hope fill you with all joy and peace as you trust in Him so that you may overflow with hope by the power of the Holy Spirit.
ROMANS 15:13

You and I have DNA that is hardwired for hope. When God created Adam and Eve in the Garden of Eden, He created them in His own image. Because of this fact, you and I have available to us the very character of God, and the verse above, Romans 15:13, tells us that one of the characteristics of our Lord is hope. No other living, breathing creature, except humans, was created to have hope.

I like to envision you and me as having a "hope meter" inside of us that registers our level of hope at any given time. A woman on her wedding day or anticipating the birth of her first child is full of hope for the future. A man beginning a new job or task is filled with hope that he will complete it with excellence. On the other hand, people who receive a doctor's diagnosis that they have a fatal disease and less than three months to live may experience their hope meter plummet to the bottom.

None of us can survive long without hope. During America's Great Depression, beginning in 1929, wealthy men jumped out of buildings to their death, because their fortunes were gone and they had lost hope. Life seemed simpler in those days, because most Americans didn't have a lot to lose. We were, by and large, an agrarian society of farmers and laborers. My mom told me that her family was already poor and life was hard; it just got a little harder during the Depression.

Today's society is vastly different. Everything we desire is available, and most of us are not accustomed to doing without. For example, money seems not to be a problem for most people who have credit cards. The struggles begin when the credit cards are maxed out and there is no money to make even the minimum payments each month. Personal finances are just one factor that can drive our hope meter to the top one day and to the bottom the next.

We live in a volatile time when nothing is certain. The economy is shaky, and unemployment is high. In decades past, the men went to work and their wives stayed home and raised the children. People knew how to grow food, so they were able to eat during hard times. Today, most families find that they require two incomes; and when either the husband or wife loses a job, family life is thrown into chaos.

Today's Hard Questions

Most of us have more questions today than answers. Will we have money to retire when the time comes? What if we get sick and have no health insurance? How will we take care of our aging parents? Many of us are so strapped for cash that we are thrown into crisis mode if our car breaks down. Most people live from paycheck to paycheck with little or no money put away for emergencies. Living in this kind of environment causes our hope meter to plummet on a fairly regular basis.

My car has an orange light that flashes when the fuel in my gas tank is low, and the flashing light alerts me that I need to stop and buy gas. In the same way, we as humans have a gauge that alerts us when our hope meter is almost empty. When it is low, we are full of feelings of despair and fear of the future. We become anxious and don't know what to do next. Sometimes we "cope" by turning to behaviors that are unhealthy, such as overeating. Or we feel so down that we discontinue behavior patterns that are healthy, such as exercising, or participating in a community of believers or praying to God. The couch suddenly seems like an inviting place to "cope," even in weather that's ideal for a vigorous and stress-relieving stroll. The bed seems like a place to "cope" on a Sunday morning, even when a community of believers who also struggle may be only a few miles away and we could encourage each other with our presence.

At First Place 4 Health, we emphasize balance in the physical, mental, emotional and spiritual areas of life. Sometimes these four areas are a little hard to separate and distinguish from one another, especially when our hope meter is out of whack.

I am a fairly hope-filled person, but there was a time when my hope meter was somewhere between low and empty. It was 1984, and we were in a desperate state. The problems began in 1981, when the oil industry seemed to dry up overnight. Because the Texas economy hinges on the energy sector, we were one of the first states hit during that time of inflation. Interest rates on mortgages were at an all-time high. People with interest rates of 17 to 18 percent had to walk away from their homes when they were unable to sell them and couldn't make the payments on the mortgage (similar to what is happening today). Houston, Texas, where we live, was full of subdivisions with several For Sale signs on every block. The economy had dried up and people were losing their jobs and were unable to find new ones. Many people left Texas during that time, hoping to find work in another location.

My husband, Johnny, owned a forklift company. In December 1980, business was good, with lots of sales and plenty of service work. But in January 1981, everything seemed to change overnight, and sales dropped drastically. Companies were cutting back and laying off workers. We struggled along from 1981 until 1984, with barely enough money to pay our mechanics plus our interest payments at the bank on the forklifts we were unable to sell but were keeping in inventory.

During that time, our youngest child was in college, and we had the added expenses of tuition plus room and board for him. Between college expenses and the overwhelming costs of keeping a business afloat in a downward-spiraling economy, we ended up going into bankruptcy and losing everything except our home.

My life was a mess during that period of time, and I was bankrupt in more ways than one. Spiritually, I was so hopeless that I didn't even pray. Even though I had become a Christian at the age of 12, my life had been controlled by me, for the most part. Our circumstances were now totally out of my control. Bill collectors called all the time, and those were the days before we used answering machines, so we couldn't avoid them.

I was embarrassed because of all that we were going through, so I made sure that very few people knew about it. Today, I still can't believe that my First Place 4 Health class didn't have a clue as to what we were experiencing. We had lost our cars, so someone had to give me a ride to work; yet I was too proud to even ask for prayer.

I've always had a strong constitution, as my mother used to call it, but during that time, I literally couldn't think straight. I didn't know what to do, so I did nothing.

A Red-letter Day

I was as close to hopeless as I have ever been when I went to church one Sunday morning in December 1984. I remember where I was sitting as if it were yesterday. That Sunday was one of those "red-letter days" that's indelibly imprinted in my mind and heart. I was hopeless; but the God of hope showed up in my life that day.

Our pastor, Dr. John Bisagno, preached a sermon on the human will that I will never forget. He said that God is a perfect gentleman who will never come in and work on our will without our permission. He said, "If you are unwilling for God to work on your stubborn will, you can pray this prayer: 'Lord, I am not willing, but I am willing to be made willing.'" This gives God permission to come in and begin the work that needs to be done.

I didn't go forward that morning for prayer, because I was on staff at the church and didn't want to have a total meltdown in front of everyone who knew me. But as sincerely as I have ever prayed a prayer, I prayed this one: "Lord, here is where I am. Until now, I've not been willing for You to make the changes that need to be made in my life. But I am hurting so much that I now pray for You to *make* me willing to be made willing, and please don't let it hurt too bad!"

Little did I know that the God of hope had just stepped back into my bleak picture. My circumstances didn't change quickly, but everything else began to change, beginning the very next day. My God didn't wait to come in to take control until I felt better; He came in right when my hope meter was at its lowest point.

As I gave God the reins of my life, He began to bring order back into it. We began crawling out of debt little by little each month until we were back on our feet financially. It didn't happen overnight. In fact, it took several years; but as we worked hard and were obedient with the money we had, God helped us heal financially.

I am forever grateful for that awful time in my life, because God used it to draw me to Himself. He also used it to teach me about money and how we spend it. He used it to lead us into debt-free living today so that we don't have to be terrified about our lives. He used it to teach us about giving back to Him a portion of everything He gives to us.

Over the years, God has continued to teach me the truth about Himself through my Bible study and memorization of His Word. He has taught me that I can be strong emotionally, not because I am a tower of strength, but because He is.

The Source of My Hope

Since those years, Johnny and I have gone through much tougher times than we did in the 1980s, yet we still have hope. Johnny has been battling stage IV prostate cancer since 1997. My mom lived with us from 1999 to 2003, and we went through so much pain watching her lose her health and mental capacity. Our 39-year-old daughter, Shari, was killed by a drunk driver in 2001, leaving a devoted husband and three darling daughters without a wife and mother who had filled their lives as she'd filled ours. And we lost our home and all of our possessions to Hurricane Ike in 2008.

It is certainly not because of any innate strength we possess that we are sane and walking upright today. It is only because our Lord keeps filling and refilling us with hope that we can stand strong and remain full of hope and peace.

God has proven Himself real to me on so many occasions that today I am full of hope, even during the toughest of trials. God's plan is to fill our "hope meter" with Himself, because He is the God of hope.

God began to teach me that my hope can never rely on circumstances or depend on the things I possess. My hope must always be placed in Him.

What does your hope meter register today? Whether it's full to the brim or close to empty, I am praying that the truths God has taught me about hope will also fill you with all joy and peace as you trust in Him, so that you will overflow with hope by the power of the Holy Spirit.

More Real-life Stories

Throughout *Hope 4 You* I will share examples of people who inspire and motivate me. Many chapters include more than one story. All real-life stories illustrate the chapter's principles. Some tell about the person's background and progress with the First Place 4 Health program, including before and after photos, if weight loss is a big factor in that person's story. (If you're interested in more success stories, go to our website, which is updated often with exciting first-person accounts of people who are putting God first every day and discovering His plan for their lives, including the four areas of health: emotional, spiritual, mental, physical.)

Later in this book you'll find a whole chapter on First Place 4 Health success stories. Meanwhile, I couldn't wait to share this one with you. It's by one of our awesome leaders, Janet Kirkhart, who also serves as the First Place 4 Health networking leader for Ohio. I know you'll love it!

Perseverance: Our Story

By Janet Kirkhart

I want to tell you not "my story" but "our story"—God's and mine—about how He has helped me to persevere!

God has changed me in so many ways. He has changed my heart and made me a different person from the inside out. He has done marvelous work in the spiritual, emotional and mental areas of my life as He works to make me more Christlike. But *the physical area has been the most difficult for me* (not for God—just for me)!

I have been in First Place 4 Health for almost 16 years, and I love the program. God has taught me so much during this time. I continue to thank and praise Him daily for the work He continues to do in my life. My journey has been one of losing weight, gaining weight and beginning again. But, through it all, God has been faithful! He has always been there ready to forgive my disobedience and give me another chance to begin again. My walk with my Savior has proven to me that I can trust Him and that, even though I may lose a battle or two (and believe me, I have), *we will win this war!*

I had severe colitis and had to go on a medical disability leave from my teaching position. My doctors told me that once a person has colitis there is really no cure; you must learn to control it or just live with it. I was taking four medications just to be able to go anywhere. And I was overweight and miserable.

I discovered First Place 4 Health in the fall of 1993, and I started leading a group the following spring. I loved the program from the very beginning because it was so balanced, and it worked for me. The Bible studies were wonderful, and I learned to have a daily quiet time for the first time in my Christian walk. I lost 65 to 70 pounds and was well on my way to my goal weight. I then developed arthritis in my knee and tendonitis in my heel. I was taking a prescription drug and over-the-counter medications just to keep going. It was difficult to exercise. Many times while attending the First Place 4 Health Wellness Week at Round Top, Texas, I could barely climb the stairs and could not do a lot of exercises with the group.

In 1998, I found myself in a three-year period that Bible teacher and author Beth Moore calls "a season of loss." I lost seven of my close family members. I had to move back to my parents' family farm where I grew up to become caregiver to my father (who was my best friend and hero) and then to my mother. I am an only child, and we were a very close family. The farm is 30 miles from my church family, my daughter's family and my friends. So, because I am an emotional and stress eater, during this time I regained almost all of the weight I had lost. But again, God was so faithful. He was with me all the time.

When I heard Carole Lewis present the "Triple Dare" at Wellness Week in October 2001, I knew that God was giving me another chance to begin. I told Carole that God had given her the Triple Dare challenge and the *Back on Track* book so that she could give them to me! I began my first Triple Dare Challenge that day! (I did four of them.) I lost 87 pounds and four dress sizes, and I was able to buy regular sizes and quit shopping the plus-size departments.

Wow—what a victory that was! I praise God for how He used this to change my life. But God was not finished yet.

During the years 2005 to 2008, I had gone up and down the scales with the same 15 to 20 pounds and continued to struggle with the physical area. During this time, God taught me some important lessons about myself. He taught me that sugar is my "trigger food" that starts me overeating, especially ice cream. I have learned to say, "Stop it!" to eating added sugar (*Stop It!* is the title of a book by Carole Lewis).

I also struggled with exercising on a regular basis. I have arthritis, which makes it difficult yet even more important that I exercise regularly. Because I have a slow metabolism, I cannot lose weight unless I eat right *and* exercise.

God also taught me that I must learn to say no (or "stop it") to allowing other people and circumstances to sidetrack me from following my commitments faithfully. There were times when I've wanted to just quit—to give up and take the easy way out.

As a First Place 4 Health leader and a networking leader, I felt unworthy. I felt that I was not being a good testimony for my Lord. In fact, I tried several times to tell Carole that although I was a "lifer" in the First Place 4 Health program, I could not continue to be a leader.

God had other plans! One year at Wellness Week, God spoke *very* plainly: "I have called you, and we will win this battle, Janet, if you will continue to trust Me and obey My plans for your life." I now know *that I know* that God has called me to this ministry, and I refuse to allow Satan to stop me as I seek God for strength and power for the victory.

One of my favorite promises that God has given me is found in Jeremiah 29:11,13: " 'For I know the plans I have for you,' declares the LORD, 'plans to prosper you and not to harm you, plans to give you hope and a future. . . . You will seek me and find me when you seek me with all your heart.' "

In 2009, we asked our First Place 4 Health members to "give God a year" (*Give God a Year* is also the title of one of

Carole's books). Carole challenged us to give God a year to do what only He can do in our lives.

Here's a summary of just a few of the amazing things God has done in my life and why "our story" (God's and mine) is all about His love and faithfulness and my perseverance, because He enables me to keep on doing what He helps me to do. I want to tell you these things to encourage you that God can do the same kind of things for you.

1. I have learned to enjoy a daily quiet time and to journal my prayers and praises.
2. God has healed the colitis that doctors said could not be healed. I do not have to take medication.
3. He healed the arthritis and tendonitis. Now I can go up and down stairs and exercise—again, no medication.
4. Remember that three-year season of loss? God has healed the emotional scars from that time and given me a level of peace and joy I've never known before—even through the difficult circumstances we all face.
5. He has continued to work miracles in my marriage. Kenny and I celebrated our forty-fifth anniversary in November 2010.
6. I received a great wellness report at last year's First Place 4 Health Wellness Week, plus good blood tests from my doctor. I feel better and younger than I did 20 years ago.
7. God brought into my life first Dr. Richard Couey, through First Place 4 Health, and used him to teach me a plan of nutrition and fitness to get rid of the arthritis. Then He introduced Dr. Gary Huber from the Lavalle Metabolic In-

stitute. Both Dr. Couey and Dr. Huber have been keynote speakers for two years at our amazing Wellness Conferences in Loveland, Ohio. Dr. Huber discovered several hormone imbalances in me and taught me what to do to correct them.

8. This year, God has definitely done amazing things in my life in the physical area! I have lost 53 pounds, making it a total of 114 pounds since I started First Place 4 Health. I am about 5 to 10 pounds from my healthy weight goal. I have gone from a size 22 to a size 10/12. We have a Body and Soul Christian aerobic ministry at our church. This past winter, part of the routine included kickboxing moves, and *I did them!* At Wellness Week, I did all the exercises twice a day (even boot camp). All of my fitness scores were above average for my age (except for balance).

I am beginning my second Give God a Year challenge, and I can hardly wait to see what He plans to do this coming year. God has taught me to be willing to give Him all the time He needs to change me from the inside out—to make me and mold me into what He wants me to be. I praise His holy name and give Him all the glory for what He has done and is doing.

Recently, Janet sent this update as to how her current efforts have been going with giving God a year:

What an amazing year 2010 has been! I started my second Give God a Year challenge, and He has already done more than I could have ever imagined. As of August 1, I have reached my ideal weight goal—the one God and I set many years ago. Not only that, but I am at my ideal BMI and percent of body fat. *I can hardly believe it!* I also just went shopping for a new outfit (one that actually fits), and I am in a size that I have *never* worn before, not even as a teenager. I have now lost a total of 7 dress sizes, 130 pounds, and just received the best medical test results of my entire life. Isn't God great! When I finally gave God *His* way and allowed *Him* to control every area of my life, He was there. He has always done His part, and He has asked me to be faithful, to persevere and to do my part.

The second real-life story is by a man named Kevin Eckert, a youth pastor at a church. I'm grateful for his candor in how the First Place 4 Health program has affected him in all four areas—the physical, the emotional, the mental and the spiritual. Kevin is a great role model of success!

One-hundred-fifty Pounds Lighter . . . and Counting

By Kevin Eckert

In 2003, I weighed approximately 450 pounds. It's a guess, because I wasn't weighing myself. In 2008, I joined First Place 4 Health. It's nearly May 2010, and I've just gone under the 300-pound mark. In fact, I weigh 299. It feels good just to be able to type that number!

But I'm getting ahead of myself. First, some background . . .

A few years ago, my wife wanted to take her little sister to Six Flags Great America, which is about halfway between Milwaukee and Chicago. (That's the closest Six Flags park to where we live in Freeport, Illinois, where I serve as youth pastor at a church.) I was looking forward to a day of fun on the rides. I was excited because I totally enjoyed the rides as a teen growing up in New Jersey, where I went to Six Flags Great Adventure.

After arriving at the Great America park, we waited in line for several hours to get on a popular roller coaster ride called the Raging Bull. When our turn came to climb into our seats, I plopped down and discovered I didn't fit. I pulled on the harness, hoping for at least one click. My brain was racing. *Oh, Lord! Now what do I do? Everyone is looking at me.*

So I got up, apologized to the attendant and left the ride—devastated and mortified.

I think I left a piece of my soul on that ride. It may sound stupid, but I'll never forget that moment. Maybe you can relate in some way. Maybe your problem is that you not only didn't fit into a normal-sized seat, but you also didn't fit into a group. I was changed that day, feeling like I needed to leave the park immediately. I was miserable.

I tried to diet after that, but for those of you who have battled the bulge, you know what a never-ending battle it is. I gave up for several years. At one point my parents wanted me to talk with others they knew had struggled with health complications from obesity. They wanted me to get better. I told them I would just die young. I'm sure they were appalled at me—and my attitude—which lasted from the summer of 2003 through late 2007. I just didn't care about my size, my aches or going on amusement park rides. (Whenever I flew, I cheerfully purchased two airline tickets.)

In late 2007, something inside me shifted. I wanted to change. I needed to change.

At first, I tried to work out, but the holidays hit and I just fell off the wagon . . . until one day in March 2008. I saw a sign at my daughter's preschool that advertised the First Place 4 Health faith-based weight-loss program. I knew I saw that sign for a reason. I went home and told my wife that I wanted to join. I asked if she would do it with me, because I knew we would make a great team.

She was excited, and so First Place 4 Health is where my journey of change began. We followed the program, and with God's help, I was able to make some awesome changes in my life.

In addition to a more than 150-pound weight loss, I would describe the change inside as "complete restoration." Before this, I had suffered from what I call closet depression. I was fairly bummed out most of the time, but only the people closest to me knew it. Now that I have learned how to give God first place in my life by handing over full control to Him—mentally, emotionally, spiritually *and* physically—I've become a very happy person. I feel truly blessed.

The First Place 4 Health group my wife and I meet with each week totally supports us; and my wife has lost 80 pounds herself. It's like a little family get-together when we see them each week. They heard my stories; and at some point, I mentioned that I wanted to get back on the rides at Six Flags Great America. When I'd lost 100 pounds, we had a celebration, and my First Place 4 Health group gave Kirsten and me tickets to Great America. I was blown away and overjoyed at how they honored my weight loss. It's one of the most touching things that's ever happened in my life. I got all choked up. I honestly almost lost it.

I look forward to getting on those rides and taking back what I left there in the summer of 2003.

I also can't wait to see the look on my mom's face when I step off that airplane at Christmas!

In this chapter, I described my concept of a "hope meter." I didn't have to go far to find an in-the-flesh example of someone whose hope meter soared to new heights. I'm a proud grandmother of Tal, who made a perfect score, 180, on his Law School Admission Test (LSAT). What follows is a conversation with Lisa, my daughter-in-law and Tal's mother, to share with readers of *Hope 4 You*.

The Story of Tal Lewis

Carole: I remember when we got the news that Tal's grade on the LSAT was the top score possible. How did that affect your hope meter?

Lisa: It skyrocketed! Before that, it was up and down. I was worried that he might be disappointed.

Carole: Oh, come on! You knew Tal would make a good grade!

Lisa: I knew it would be good, because he's such a conscientious student. But he puts a lot of pressure on himself. Before the exam that counted, he would take a practice test every other day, and each time his score would be different.

Carole: What a blessing that he made a perfect score when it counted! According to the Law School Admissions Council, only about 30 students—or 2 percent of the people who took the LSAT—scored a 180.

Lisa: Tal is so motivated and, as a mother, I feel protective of him. He was thinking about a career in law as early as high school where he excelled in debate. Now he's finishing his undergraduate degree at the University of Texas at Austin with a triple major. He's also completed an internship with Texas House Representative Dora Olivo, where he became interested in how law affects society.

Carole: A politician in the making?

Lisa: He says the purpose of law is making sure that society is fair and just. I know Tal will serve God with his career just as he does with his life.

For Study

1. Take a few minutes to reflect on the concept of your internal hope meter. A simplified way to think of it is to imagine the fuel gauge on your car's dashboard. Some of us wait until the needle is pointing to E (Empty) before pulling in to a gas station for a fill-up. Keep in mind that there's nothing really wrong with waiting that long before going to your source for refueling—*when it comes to vehicles and gasoline*. In fact, I've heard from mechanics that it's a good idea occasionally to empty your gas tank. On the other hand, there are times when it's beneficial to keep the gas tank close to full, like in winter conditions when you need the additional weight in your car to maintain good traction. (But, hey, don't service your car according to *my* advice—the hope meter I imagine in my mind just happens to look like my car's fuel gauge!)

   Go to the first drawing of a "hope meter" in this study section and draw an arrow at the location that best describes your *overall* level of hope. Jot a few notes about what prompted your notation of a personal hope meter that seems full, or squarely at the one-quarter mark, or just plain empty—whatever level fits your circumstances. Place today's date beside the hope meter.

2. Now let's break this down into categories. At First Place 4 Health, we view hope as affecting all four areas of life—the heart, the soul, the mind and the body. Stated differently, we seek balance in life in these four ways: emotionally, spiritually, mentally and physically. Sometimes it's hard to separate these areas. In this chapter "The Source of Hope," I shared my hus-

band's and my story of financial failure, even going through bankruptcy in the 1980s. But this was a problem that affected Johnny and me far beyond our bank account:

- I was also spiritually bankrupt, unable to ask my First Place 4 Health group for prayer because of my pride, and unable to admit that I had not given God the reins of my life, because I wouldn't admit weakness in front of a church where I served in a staff position (spiritual imbalance).
- The pain of loss for our company, its employees and all that we had worked for was heartbreaking, causing me fits of weeping and a loss of confidence (emotional imbalance).
- Although I'm naturally of a logical bent and effective at problem-solving, this situation was so overwhelming that I literally could not think straight (mental imbalance).
- And there's no telling what the stress was doing to my physical health—to my body (physical imbalance).

As I write *Hope 4 You*, we are still experiencing what many call the Great Recession. No, we don't have bread lines like history shows us existed in the 1930s. But businesses are cutting expenses, and that means layoffs. Families and individuals are making do on less—often *much* less. Investments are low; I recently heard a friend refer to his 401(k) as a 201(k).

Your situation might be different. Perhaps you are weathering the recession with a steady income and good financial management, but you have a sick spouse; a child who doesn't know the Lord as his or her Savior; or responsibilities for an elderly parent. (Conversely, you may be celebrating the reversal of a bad situation.)

At this point, I would like for you to quantify your circumstances, using the following four hope meter drawings and the spaces provided for jotting notes. This will provide a benchmark for any changes in the future, so be sure to date it. Feel free to use whatever terminology works for you. Let's say your son recently announced his engagement to a woman with strong Christian faith, after years of dating that wouldn't have resulted in an "equally yoked" match. You may want to categorize that as "parenting," or you may prefer to use the First Place 4 Health categories to illustrate how that one victory affects you emotionally, spiritually, mentally and physically. Or perhaps you are struggling with credit card debt. If so, you will want to note that circumstance, again using a term that's meaningful to you, or—if you're ready—the First Place 4 Health terminology.

So make this exercise work for you by personalizing it!

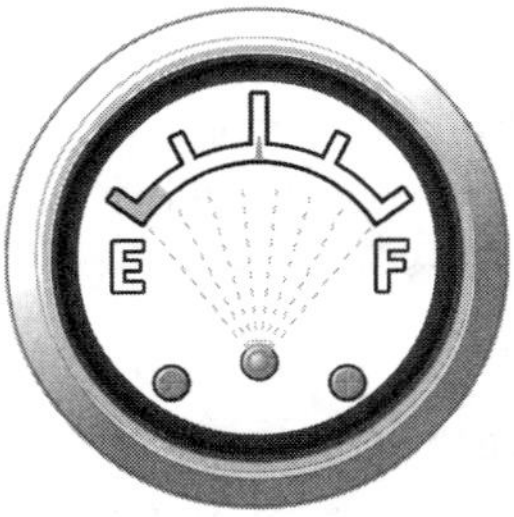

3. Fill in the missing words from the Bible verse at the beginning of this chapter:

   May the God of hope ________ you with all joy and peace as you ____________in______, so that you may overflow with hope by the ________________of the _____________ ___________ (Rom. 15:13).

   Your hope meter(s) serves as a visual gauge, perhaps a list of praises and prayer requests. What does Romans 15:13 tell you about your *real* source of hope?

Heavenly Father, help me to understand a concept that surely You authored—balance in my heart, soul, mind and body. As I read this book and study its principles, show me how I can find this balance through You. Amen.

2

Building a Fortress Around Hope

But the worries of this life, the deceitfulness of wealth and the desires for other things come in and choke the word, making it unfruitful.
MARK 4:19

When I wrote the first chapter of this book, I was full of hope. I had given a message on hope several times in the previous months, and the outline for the book had come from that message. I believed that God had placed the desire to write this book into my heart, and so I was up and ready for the task. I even took a week of vacation at Thanksgiving so that I could spend the time writing.

I thoroughly enjoyed that week with Johnny, but I was unable to get one word of the book written. Even though I got up early every morning, as I always do, there was *nothing* happening with the writing of this book. Thanksgiving came and went, and by the time I returned to work on Monday, my hope meter was nearly on empty.

When I left work that afternoon, I had a feeling the staff was glad to see me go. And why wouldn't they be—I was dragging down everyone's usually good mood! All day I'd joked about the fact that I have to write a book on hope, and yet I have no hope that I'll be able to write the book. They laughed at my lame attempt at humor, but I was truly feeling hopeless that the book was going to happen.

This morning, at 1:20 A.M., I awoke with the verse for this chapter going through my mind, and I instantly realized what had happened to my hope. The last few weeks had been full of "the worries of this life." My mind had been distracted with thoughts of where we were going to live and how much work it would be to furnish a new home.

A Worry "Blows" In

When Hurricane Ike destroyed our home on Galveston Bay—and blew away our household possessions—we obviously had an immediate problem on our hands. The first answer came in the form of an invitation from our dear friends—Nick and Euphanel Goad. They own a beautiful and roomy retreat center on acreage near a small historic town named Round Top, in Texas, about an hour east of Austin. Their center includes one large building designed like a lovely old rambling home (although it was built in the 1980s), and other smaller but very comfortable houses.

This retreat center is the location for our annual fall Wellness Week where First Place 4 Health members and others gather to learn about and experience a healthy lifestyle. The week includes food planning, exercise and healing in all the areas we address: physical, mental, emotional and spiritual. (Of course, the setting includes a barn—what Texans with acreage wouldn't have a barn!—so that's where we do our group physical workouts.)

Naturally, Johnny and I always feel comfortable and at home at the Goads' inviting retreat center, but little did we know it would actually become our home for five weeks after the hurricane. It was a wonderful setting for us to simply think, recall and organize ourselves for what was to be our next onslaught: dealing with insurance adjusters. When your home has been ripped to smithereens, and your possessions blown into Galveston Bay, the next flood you must deal with involves paperwork, meetings, phone calls and the tracking of details almost beyond comprehension.

We were blessed with people to help us, such as our daughter Lisa, who—besides being a great cook—set up an Excel spreadsheet so that we could list items lost as we remembered them from every room (including each object in that room's cabinets, closets, drawers, and so forth). Becky Turner, who has fabulous organizational skills, showed me how to make a tab in my planner, which became an indispensible tool for keeping track of the large cast of characters—ranging from insurance personnel to government agencies—who would dominate our attention for what seemed like forever.

Soon we had to return to pick through the debris, a heartbreaking task. Our time in Round Top had been just what we needed at the Goads' retreat center (which brought new meaning to the word "retreat" since the aftermath of Hurricane Ike felt like a mighty army had attacked our home, ravaging everything in its path).

We were able to rent a home from our neighbors whose home survived the hurricane because it was newer and built on pilings. So we left Round Top with all of our worldly possessions, which easily fit into my car and Johnny's truck and included two cat carriers, one birdcage and our dog, Meathead, and headed back to Galveston Bay. From the rented home, we supervised the process of tearing down what was left of our house. We also met with insurance adjusters and other people who get involved in the disaster-relief process after a hurricane.

"The worries of this life." It's an understatement to say Hurricane Ike was a "worry." But the days ahead were filled with worries, and like a mighty storm they sucked the hope out of me—because I let them.

How Do You Build a Fortress?

One lesson I learned from the hurricane is that you can't build a fortress around things. Oh, sure, a house facing Galveston Bay can be built on pilings, which helps a lot with strong winds and a storm surge. But it doesn't prevent a hurricane with the force of Ike from leaving devastation in its path.

Our house looked like the other homes of the same vintage in the neighborhood, completely gutted from the surge of water that undoubtedly poured in and out, sweeping everything—from walls to furnishings—into the bay. Our pier was gone, and so was the large deck over our boat lift. We again picked through the debris, as we had during our brief trip right after the storm when we found items like half of the headboard of our bed. It was sad and yet symbolic of the futility of expecting to be able to build a fortress around belongings. As if to underscore that lesson, the entire fence that had surrounded our property was missing, now shattered into toothpicks and blown to sea.

The plain and simple fact was this: After taking care of what we could, it was time to move on. We were able to return to Houston in time for Christmas, where we rented a lovely furnished townhouse from our friend Linda. There we could get back to the important business of building a fortress around our *hope*.

One of the first signs to me that this process of "moving on" had begun was that soon after returning to Houston, Johnny's strength began returning. But we still had to be realistic. As I've already shared with you, Johnny was diagnosed in 1997 with stage IV prostate cancer. Since then, a major boost to our hope has been the many years he's lived beyond the dismal predictions doctors gave us in the first years of Johnny's battle. However, stress ("the worries of this life") has a negative effect on cancer patients. So we had some decisions to make beyond just how to get a permanent roof over our heads. How could we accomplish this without adding to our stress? Should we rebuild on the coast or simply establish a new home in Houston?

As we considered our circumstances, the latter began to seem like God's plan for us. For example, we'd purchased a used RV to put on our property at the bay so we could go there to stay overnight or for a weekend. But it's been a real job trying to get electricity and water restored to the property, and—as of the writing of this book—it still hasn't happened. We've made at least five trips to the bay, and the "fifth wheel" is still parked on the driveway—unused. With Johnny's upcoming months of chemo treatments, something we really aren't looking forward to, we were beginning to realize that the Lord was nudging us toward establishing a full-time residence in Houston.

Coming to grips with this has been hard. We have a strong attraction to the water—as a restful location for us, as a couple growing older and as a vacation home for our children and grandchildren. What we had was not enormous or extravagant. In fact, it was modest compared to many homes on the bay. But, while writing this book, I've had a chance to reflect back on the factors that led to our decision to live full-time in Houston (keeping our now cleared property on the bay, of course). I see the Lord's hand in the process at every turn.

How Does It Feel to Lose Hope?

Many of you who know me personally are aware that I've never considered myself a writer of books. I never wanted to write a book, because I knew it would take many hours that I would rather spend playing. Every book that I've written has been a true God project from beginning to end, and I knew that if God didn't write this book through me, it just wasn't going to happen. My hope meter—on all four levels—was precarious at best. One day the mental gymnastics of dealing with insurance matters would appear to be over and done with; the next day, I would learn of much more information I had to supply. The emotional tug of missing our beautiful view, and the ability to go for a boat ride at the drop of a hat, would have me in tears one day, yet upbeat the next because of the close proximity to family and work that a home in Houston would provide. I could go on, describing the physical and spiritual roller coaster from despair to joy and back down to despair again, sometimes within a single day. The plain truth, however, is that I felt hopeless more than I felt hopeful.

In retrospect, I believe that God wanted me to see what it feels like to lose hope at the time I had a contract to write a book on that very subject. I'm not implying that God caused Hurricane Ike to make landfall right at our home on Galveston Bay, but He allowed it. And I'm not implying that He caused the timing of that and the critical aftermath of chaotic activities, which came just before the anniversary of our daughter's death at Thanksgiving. But again, He allowed it.

At this point, you may be thinking, *Wow, Carole, you've already revealed to us that you and Johnny lost everything in the hurricane, that Johnny has cancer and that you've had tremendous grief to bear—such as the looming anniversary of the death of your daughter Shari, who was killed by a drunk driver. With all of these things pressing on you while you were trying to write a book on hope, why wouldn't you feel down?*

I would agree. It sounds like a prescription for hopelessness. And feeling hopeless is part of the human condition from time to time. God created us to be emotional beings. The point is: He provided us with a way out of that sense of hopelessness. Yet, all of us have to find that path; and if it were easy, we wouldn't need God.

It is fascinating to me how God has ordered my steps along that path, and it is a joy to be able to share them with you. I have already told you about waking up with this chapter's Scripture verse running through my head. Now God used something else.

God Reminds Me of a Hymn

I am normally a person who is full of hope, so I was clueless about what to do with the feelings of hopelessness I'd been experiencing recently. For me, it became a sort of malaise that was all over me from the time I woke up until I went to sleep at night. I was doing all the "right things," like reading my Bible and praying about the problem, but what had happened was that the "worries of this life" had come in and choked the Word, making it unfruitful.

Finally, an old hymn began running through my mind, one of God's very personalized ways of showing me a biblical truth. It was "The Solid Rock" by Edward Mote. That hymn reminded me that my fortress of protection to prevent me from sinking into hopelessness *always* must be built on Jesus. As I've learned, no physical "fortress" exists to protect us from devastation like the winds of a hurricane or the storm surge that follows.

I have sung the words to "The Solid Rock" over and over, because they are true and they ultimately draw me back to Jesus:

My hope is built on nothing less
Than Jesus' blood and righteousness.
I dare not trust the sweetest frame,
but wholly lean on Jesus' name.

On Christ, the solid Rock, I stand
All other ground is sinking sand,
All other ground is sinking sand.[1]

You and I will go through times when our hope meter is seriously depleted. The secret to restoring hope is to finally realize that our hope is not found in anything but Jesus Christ, who, according to His words in Mark 4:19, understands our emotional stressors even in the twenty-first century. His blood (and the righteousness it provides us) is the *specific fortress* around our hope. When we lose sight of that fact, our hope begins to fade. Of course we occasionally feel hopeless; but if we review His words and the meaning of the sacrifice He made for us, we can pull out of that deep emotional pit.

Rick Warren's Focus on Purpose

Rick Warren wrote the book *The Purpose Driven Life*, which has sold more than 30 million copies. Rick is pastor of Saddleback Church, in Southern California, and I'm quite sure he never dreamed when he wrote the book how wildly successful it would be. Recently, I read an interview that Paul Bradshaw did with Rick Warren, and it was chock-full of wisdom that Rick has learned since becoming instantly wealthy and famous. I want to share with you some of what Rick said.

When people ask Rick what he believes is the purpose of life, he tells them that life is preparation for eternity, adding that people were created to last forever and that God wants us to be with Him in heaven. He calls our time on earth the warm-up act for the trillions of years we will spend in eternity—the "dress rehearsal." According to Rick, "God wants us to practice on earth what we will do forever in eternity."[2]

Rick goes on to say that life is a series of problems, meaning we're always either in the throes of a problem, coming out of one or preparing to go into another one. God allows them because He is more interested in our character than our comfort. Our heavenly

Father, who always knows and wants the best for us, is more interested in our becoming holier than our becoming happier.

Rick shared in the interview that the past year had been the greatest and the toughest year of his life. His wife, Kay, had been diagnosed with cancer, and even though it had been difficult for her, God had strengthened her character, given her a ministry of helping other people and drawn her closer to Him.

What Rick said next really ministered to my heart and resonated in my soul:

> I used to think that life was hills and valleys—you go through a dark time, then you go to the mountaintop, back and forth. I don't believe that anymore. Rather than life being hills and valleys, I believe that it's kind of like two rails on a railroad track, and at all times you have something good and something bad in your life. No matter how good things are in your life, there is always something bad that needs to be worked on. And no matter how bad things are in your life, there is always something good you can thank God for.[3]

You won't be surprised to learn that this pastor and author, who has branded the concept of purpose-driven living, added that people can focus on their problems or their purpose. People who choose to focus on their problems are, by definition, being self-centered, because they are thinking of *their* issues and *their* pain. He recommends adjusting our focus onto God and others, which also turns our attention away from ourselves and life's inevitable problems.

The Worries of This Life

Mark 4:19 lists three distractions that "choke the Word, making it unfruitful":

- The worries of this life
- The deceitfulness of wealth
- The desire for other things

I believe the first of these, the worries of this life, is the primary reason we lose hope. For me, the key word is "worries." We all have a list of problems going on in our life at any given time. We lose hope when we begin focusing on the problems ("worrying") instead of focusing on the Problem Solver. Our God has the answer for every problem we face today.

Since Hurricane Ike, Johnny and I have wanted to be absolutely sure that we don't miss God's perfect will for us at this point in our lives. We know that He knows where we are and that He is working everything out for our good. He has taken care of our every need by providing us a furnished townhome to live in for the last year, plus many other comforts, willing and helpful people and other solutions to what, in anybody's book, would be an enormous crisis.

Yet, I realized that I had allowed my mind to become consumed with wanting a place of my own. In other words, during this second holiday season since Ike, my nesting instincts had kicked in to full tilt, and my wants and desires had robbed me of hope and joy.

Mark 4:19 pretty much sums up where I have been lately—worried about our life, where we will live and what we will do. It's an unfounded worry when I analyze it logically and through the spiritual eyes of my faith. We are certainly not wealthy, but we do have the insurance money from the storm, even if we are still uncertain what specifically is God's will for the use of that money. If we are to buy a home in town, rather than rebuild at the bay, how do we go about doing that? It's daunting! But now that I ponder Mark 4:19, I recognize why I have been stuck in that hopeless feeling of neutral. God will reveal to us His step-by-step solution, and it will draw us closer to Him and His plans for our future.

The Deceitfulness of Wealth

In the interview with Rick Warren, he spoke to this fact of life, the deceitfulness of wealth, saying that we all must learn to deal with both good and bad. Dealing with the good sometimes can be harder, he added, citing the instant wealth his book brought him. It also brought notoriety, which was new to Rick, making him wonder what God wanted him to do with the money and influence. He found his answers in 2 Corinthians 9 and Psalm 72, which led to several financial choices. He and Kay decided they would not change their lifestyle one bit, despite all the money coming in. In fact, they discontinued taking a salary from Saddleback Church and even established a foundation called The Peace Plan to plant churches, equip leaders, care for the sick, assist the poor and educate the next generation. They also added up his total salary from 24 years of service at Saddleback and donated that sum back to the church, a move he described as "liberating to be able to serve God for free." According to Rick, "We need to ask ourselves, 'Am I going to live for possessions? Popularity? Am I going to be driven by pressures? Guilt? Bitterness? Materialism? Or am I going to be driven by God's purposes for my life?'"[4]

Rick Warren has learned that great wealth has the potential to rob us of everything God wants to do in our lives. Even though Johnny and I don't have great wealth, the insurance money caused me to take my eyes off Jesus and His greater purposes for us right now. This is a tricky concept in today's economy where our possessions are insured. I want to make clear that I'm not opposed to insurance as a sound business principle or life practice. However, I realize that—when insurance pays off as it did after Hurricane Ike wiped us out—it's tempting to feel secure because of the money, not because of God's daily and very personal provision.

People often think that money has the power to solve most of life's problems, but the truth is that money is deceitful and has no power to build hope into our lives. One of the richest, sweetest times in our life was when we had absolutely no money and had to rely entirely on God's provision. We found great joy in packing a sack lunch and driving to the beach. As we walked on the free sand, looked at the free ocean and savored the free sunset, we became aware that our God has provided far more for us than was necessary.

God loves you and me so much that He created a beautiful earth for us to inhabit. Most of us have a roof over our heads and electric lights. We have furniture to sit on and food to eat. We are blessed indeed.

The Desire for Other Things

Of Jesus' list of three distractions that "choke the word, making it unfruitful"—the worries of this life, the deceitfulness of wealth, and the desire for other things—this last one is a real hope robber. As I have fretted about where we will live, I also have bought a few things for the home I don't even have. I bought a set of stainless silverware and kitchen utensils. Even yesterday, I stopped by the Goodwill store on the way home and found a glass container for the utensils. You may be thinking, *So what? Those aren't extravagant purchases.* And I would agree with that assessment, unless you consider that we don't yet need even these simple items. They are furnished for us in the lovely townhome we are renting, so I can't use my purchases, and I have nowhere to store them until we get a permanent home. (So where are they? Sitting on the kitchen table, waiting for a place to be used.)

Let me assure you that I'm not beating myself up for buying a few kitchen utensils! I'm simply explaining that God has provided a townhome for us, and in it we have all that we need for now. Soon we will take the next step according to His plan. He wants us to notice that He has provided for us on a daily basis, and He wants us to trust Him for the future, or He wouldn't have arranged for "the desire for other things" to be on the list of distractions that can rob us of hope. When you think about it, Mark 4:19 gives us the formula for hopelessness: worrying about our problems, money and possessions. Because I have been caught up in all three for the last several weeks, the Word of God has been choked in my life. Even though I was still reading it and frantically studying, it was choked out by my own thoughts and behavior.

God is so patient and kind with each of us that He lets us wallow around until we get miserable enough to look up and cry out for help . . . one more time. My prayer for me as I write this book and for you as you read it is that we will never lose sight of where our hope comes from—Christ, the solid Rock. On Him we can build the foundation for our fortress around hope.

Real-life Story

Some stories are better told in the person's own voice. I'll let a man who prefers to be anonymous tell about falling into pornography addiction and his amazing story of how God lifted him out of it. I think you'll see how he was sinking fast and losing hope. It was a direct result of his behavior and how he had allowed Satan into his daily life. Eventually, by God's grace, he was able to build a fortress and, as you'll learn later in this book, begin a one-on-one ministry to other men; but not before some incredibly bad stuff seeped into his life and the life of his family.[5]

"Mitchell's" Story

> My hope came to a screeching halt in 2000. That's when my wife filed for divorce. I can't say that I blame her, when I'm honest with myself. I did something that seemed innocent enough in the beginning, but—literally within weeks—it consumed me.
>
> It started like this. I was in the habit of checking work emails from my home computer before bed. Nothing wrong with that. After the emails, I would go to the Internet for a few minutes of research, such as stock quotes, game scores, airline schedules if I had a flight coming up. Again, nothing wrong with that. It was routine.
>
> One night, I was clicking away when all of a sudden a porn site popped up. I had heard of them but never seen one. I clicked on it. My jaw almost dropped. With one click of the mouse I was viewing images that were riveting. I was there only a few seconds when I heard my wife down the hall, so I shut down the site. I realized I had stopped breathing, and my palms were sweaty. I wiped them on my pants legs and took a deep breath. I clicked back to a stock market site.

A few nights later, same routine. I was checking emails, the news, and so on. The porn site hadn't popped up again since that first time, which had been a relief. But this night was different. I felt edgy, maybe worried about something coming up at work—I don't recall. Anyway, I began to click around looking for it, of all things. Finally, I gave up and went to bed.

But the images swam in my mind during those drowsy minutes before sleep, and the next night I looked again. This time I found it. A hyperlink took me to another site and then another. It was so easy. And I wanted more.

Next time, I found a chat room. For a while, I just lurked there, "listening," learning the protocol, the rules. The protocol was to talk as dirty as possible. *Nah,* I thought. *Too weird.* But the next night I did. A few nights later a woman typed a message suggesting we meet, and I wrote back yes.

But I didn't meet her. I never met her. I thought of my wife and teenage kids and the words I'd said at the marriage altar.

The next couple of weeks were a blur. My wife seemed grouchy, but when she asked about the additional time I was spending on the computer at night, I told her, "Too little time at the office." She let it go.

Finally, I *did* meet someone. When I left the motel, I knew once would be enough. It was disgusting, and I felt like I needed a good shower. *I need to have my head examined*, is what I thought.

It was weeks before I clicked on anything more radical than the weather. But one day I fell again. By now, you're probably thinking this could never happen to you, because you're older and wiser, happily married and a Christian. But the same things applied to me.

Flash forward a few months. My wife found me out. To her credit, she gave me chance after chance to stop. I tried counseling with our associate pastor. This glimpse into one of our conversations shows how deep I was into rationalization and other stupid thinking, and his valiant effort to lift me out:

> Mitchell: I can handle this. I won't let it get out of hand.
> Pastor: Oh, really? Can you play with a cobra and not get bitten?
> Mitchell: God wants me to be happy.
> Pastor: Hm-m, I think His Word says He wants you to be holy.
> Mitchell: I don't want anybody to get hurt.
> Pastor: News flash! There's no such thing as a safe affair.

Well, of course, *everyone* got hurt. My wife and I separated. My children shunned me. I attended sex addiction rehab—twice. Between the rehabs she filed for divorce.

It took nearly a year and a half for me to redeem myself in her eyes and the kids' and, of course, in my own. When I quit lying to myself, I was so ashamed. I asked their forgiveness one member of my family at a time. Frankly, it took more than one "asking." *But God forgave me as soon as I asked Him,* and He provided me with the strength—and eventually the hope—to go on living and to reunite my family.

What I learned from the experience is that God really can and does give us power over our thoughts and impulses, but *only if we will let Him*. And now—many readjustments later (including installing a whole new computer so the old sites no longer pop up, plus additional software to block such trash)—I have a much different life and routine. For one thing, I seek the Lord every morning. My alarm is set half an hour earlier, and I begin my day with coffee, Bible study and prayer. For another, I have an accountability group of other men who have been through the same hell on earth I experienced. And, yes, I still check emails at night, plus the sports scores and so forth. I have invited my wife to come into my home office to check on me any time she wants. Because of the grace of God, she trusts me again and has never felt the need to do that.

Only God could build such a fortress.

For Study

1. Fill in the missing words from the Bible verse at the beginning of this chapter:

   But the __________________ of this life, the _____________________________ of wealth and the ____________ for other things come in and ___________ the word, making it unfruitful (Mark 4:19).

2. List some of the "worries" of your life.

   ____

   ____

   ____

   ____

   ____

   Describe an example in which you have found chasing wealth to be not as rewarding as some people think it's cracked up to be (deceitful).

   ____

   ____

   ____

   Describe an example in which your desire for "other things" has "choked the Word, making it unfruitful."

   ____

   ____

   ____

   ____

3. To build a fortress around your hope, list ways you plan to avoid all three of these pitfalls.

____

____

____

____

____

Gracious God, give me the strength to build a fortress around my hope, one that keeps me from worrying about the details of my life and prevents me from longing for wealth and other things and helps me put these into Your perspective, not mine. It is my prayer that Your Word will always be fruitful in my life. Thank You, Father. Amen.

3

Walking with God

Whether you turn to the right or to the left, your ears will hear a voice behind you saying, "This is the way; walk in it."
ISAIAH 30:21

I believe there are three essentials we must master before we will be able to live a hope-filled life. We must learn how to:

- Walk with God
- Work with God
- Wait on God

In this chapter we will endeavor to see what is involved in learning how to walk with God. (We will deal with the other two essentials in later chapters.) The reason "walk with God" is the first essential in living a hope-filled life is that we can get lost unless we learn how to walk with Him.

In my travels I've been lost a number of times, but the absolute worst time happened a few years ago when I drove to Kerrville, Texas, to speak at a women's retreat. It was late January 2005, and my friend and assistant, Pat, offered to go with me. Kerrville is only about a four-hour drive from Houston, and we had a wonderful time being together. Pat and I have been best friends for more than 30 years, and even though we work together every day, we don't get to spend a lot of time visiting. Going on a road trip like this would give us time to get caught up on everything happening in our lives.

I spoke three times to the group between Friday night and Sunday morning, so when the retreat was over that morning, I felt a little weary. The weekend had gone really well, but Pat and I were both ready to get home. It was 11:30, and even though it was lunch time, we'd had a late brunch with the group, so we decided to head for the highway.

Kerrville is west of Houston, about an hour past San Antonio. As we began driving, we talked about making sure that we turned east on I-10 to drive back to Houston. After a few miles, Pat said, "Why don't we pray and thank God for the wonderful weekend?" We began praying out loud (I kept my eyes on the road, of course!) and must have prayed a long time, because when we finished, I looked at my fuel gauge and it was past empty! I looked at my odometer and it said 90 miles. There were beautiful stone bluffs on both sides of the highway, yet we hadn't passed San Antonio, which was 66 miles from Kerrville.

Pat and I looked at each other and said, "Where in the world are we?" After a minute or two, we saw a sign telling us that Sonora was the next exit. Well . . . we had driven 90 miles west instead of east on I-10, meaning that we were only an hour or two from Del Rio and the Mexico border! The thought that we had to retrace our steps was exhausting, so we decided to take a break and eat lunch in Sonora. Then we drove an hour and a half back to Kerrville before we could even start the four-hour drive home. All in all, we drove 525 miles on what should have been a 300-mile trip!

This story has all the elements of how we must learn to walk with God if we are ever going to get to where He wants us to be as believers. The Christian life is much like a journey. We begin it the day we invite Jesus Christ to come into our life, and the journey doesn't end until Jesus calls us home.

We Need a Map

Pat and I had a Texas map when we left on our trip to Kerrville. We used the map on the trip there, but we thought we knew how to get home, so we didn't even open the map. Our map for the Christian life journey is the Bible. As a new believer, I had a great hunger to learn the truths of God's Word. Although I was just 12 years old when I became a Christian, I was immediately aware of how the Bible came to life once I became acquainted with Jesus Christ, the central character of the Book. I now had the ability to understand the truths of God's Word, because the Holy Spirit had come to take up residence inside of me the minute I met Jesus personally. It is essential that we learn what the Bible has to say about every aspect of this life on earth if we are to learn how to walk with God.

The Bible tells us exactly what to do in every situation we encounter. It gives us divine instruction about everything we will ever struggle with in this life. It tells us what to do and what not to do when we have problems with . . .

- Money
- Marriage
- Relationships
- Forgiveness
- Children
- How to live
- How to die
- Hope
- Faith
- Trust
- Love
- Sickness
- Patience
- Kindness
- Gentleness
- Our speech
- Making decisions
- Anger
- Grief
- Anxiety
- Fear
- Loneliness

I could go on and on, but you get the point: The Bible is our roadmap to life, and unless we study it to learn what it says, we will not be able to walk consistently with God. We will become hopelessly lost, sometimes to the point of feeling that we can never find our way back to walking with God again.

A side note about Pat: Her walk with the Lord is so authentic and inspiring. I've been learning from Pat for years, going way back to the 1980s when Johnny and I were navigating through treacherous financial straits. She knew us when our forklift company sank with the economy. After that we were flat broke, looking back fondly on our newlywed days in the early 1960s, when we had bought a three-bedroom house for a mere $10,700 (monthly payment: $72!). A week's worth of groceries cost $10. Johnny brought home $116 per week, yet it never seemed like we struggled to make ends meet.

Later, when we experienced bankruptcy, our business was gone. Oh, sure, we kept our house and furnishings, but not our cars.

Close friends gave us a hand up by providing jobs in their stone yard, me doing payroll and books, and Johnny selling ornamental stone. That kept us going for several months, but in all honesty, I was miserable. I'd left a job in ministry to work with Johnny in the forklift business that was now bust, and I longed to go back to ministry where I felt called. (My apologies to those of you who are passionate about forklifts and ornamental stone!) Johnny assured me that if I returned to working at the church, we could make it financially even if I took a salary cut. I called the church and was hired as a receptionist in the education department.

Enter my friend Pat. God knew she was probably the only person to whom I would listen about truth, thankfulness, money and God's plan for my life. He orchestrated events so she could tell me what He was preparing her to say. Because Johnny and I were still struggling financially, I didn't even have a car, so I depended on Pat for a ride to work at First Baptist Houston where she had been on staff for a while.

We had developed a tradition of spending a whole day shopping together at Christmas—mostly it was just a fun-filled day of being together, because I really didn't have the money to buy much. At the end of the day, Pat and I were about to part company in front of my house when she said she had something to discuss with me. Looking back, I believe God used Pat to speak the truth because of her love and loyalty to me. She said she believed that God wanted to do something really big in my life, but her fear was that I might miss it if I didn't give up control of my life to Him. My first thought was: *Control? What did that have to do with anything? Johnny and I were in debt up to our eyeballs. If anything, we needed to strike oil.*

Fortunately, Pat had earned the right to speak into my life, because her walk with God was (and is) so compelling. I heard her loud and clear—I was bankrupt in more ways than financially.

I sat right in the front seat of her car and cried. She cried with me, and then we prayed together. To illustrate how God orchestrates the details, this happened only two weeks before I heard the sermon at church about how God is a perfect gentleman when it comes to our will. That was the day I prayed: "Lord, I am not willing, but I am willing to be made willing." That was the beginning of a dramatic chain of events that led to my becoming national director of the First Place 4 Health program. What a turnaround! All because God provided a "map"—directions from His Word, a faithful friend and the Holy Spirit living inside me because of my commitment to Jesus as my Savior when I was a child.

We Need to Stay Alert

Flash ahead to the crazy road trip from Kerrville to Houston in 2005. Pat and I were doing a good thing by praying out loud on the drive back home. My eyes were open the entire time, since I was the one driving; but obviously I was not alert to what was going on around me. Had I been alert, I would have noticed that the city of San Antonio never materialized on the left side of the car, and the scenery was dramatically different from the first leg of the trip. West Texas looks entirely different from South Texas where we live.

Many times, Christ-followers are busy doing "good things," yet we still end up lost and not knowing how to get back to walking with God again. I'm acquainted with literally hundreds of people who are strong Christians, including many who are in full-time ministry work; yet even they occasionally seem to stray from the direction they intended to go. This puzzles many people, especially nonbelievers, when they learn that a Christ-follower is experiencing problems. But mature Christians know the reason this happens, and 1 Peter 5:8 gives us the answer: "Be self controlled and alert. Your enemy the devil prowls around like a roaring lion looking for someone to devour." Our enemy knows that he can never have our soul, because our soul is secure once we accept Jesus Christ into our lives. But Satan can wreak plenty of havoc. His purpose in the life of a Christian is to destroy every good thing God has planned for us. He does not have the power to read our minds, but he watches our past behavior and knows what has tripped us up in the past. If he can distract us, he has a chance of pulling us off the path of walking with God.

This also can happen if our walk with Christ has reached a plateau. Think back on my story of hearing my pastor preach on how God allows us the free will to place control of our life into His hands. That was decades after I'd made my decision to accept Jesus as my Lord and Savior, and it was years after I'd been in ministry work, surrounded by mature believers, and even after attending Bible study groups and growing in my faith. In other words, the Christian walk is a journey. (Some people like to say it's a marathon, not a sprint.) Giving up control was my next step. Being alert for the enemy's distractions was another step.

We must learn the difference between the good and the best when it comes to walking with God. West Texas is a beautiful place, but going west instead of east on Interstate 10 was never the right direction to get us home to Houston.

Sometimes We Need to Turn Around

When we get lost, it is imperative that we get out the map (our Bible), find out where we got off track and then head back in the right direction. If we have the Word of God deep inside of us, then the Holy Spirit is able to bring it up when we feel hopeless of ever getting back on the right path. Just like the other night when I woke up with Mark 4:19 playing over and over in my mind, had I not memorized this verse of Scripture, it most likely would not have been there to remind me of what was going on in my life. Once I had the answer, it was easy to turn around and get back in step with where God and I were going before I got lost.

The key is to remember that even when we feel hopelessly lost, God is not lost at all. He knows exactly where He is and where we are, and He has a purpose for everything we go through on the journey. If we have ever walked with Him, we can walk with Him again. The secret is being willing to turn around and go back to the point where we quit walking in step with Him and got lost.

Every believer will feel hopelessly lost from time to time on this journey called life. But we must not rely on our feelings. We can only rely on the truth of the map, our Bible, and the directions we will find in it to get us back on the path toward home again.

Walking with God is, without a doubt, the most exciting journey we could ever undertake. It is never boring or dull, and it is always full of challenges that demand we stay alert. The way back is not hopeless, but we can never get there until we turn around and head back in the right direction.

The most beautiful thing about the journey with Christ is that the longer we walk together, the easier it is to turn around and get back into step. Years ago, I would become so hopelessly lost in sin that I despaired of ever being able to walk close to Him again. But because of the relationship I have established with Him through the various trials and tribulations I have gone through on the journey, I now know that He has never left me and that He will never leave me. I love the way my friend and First Place 4 Health leader (and networking leader for Mississippi) Joyce Ainsworth puts it: "I believe the only way we can keep in step is to 'walk with God' daily in prayer and Bible study, always being a 'seeker' for His direction."[1]

A true Christian can never be hopelessly lost. It may feel that way, but that is a lie. If you have ever walked with Him, you can walk with Him again. Get out the map; find out where you took a wrong turn, and then turn around and go back. He is waiting to walk with you again.

Real-life Story

A friend agreed to share her story of losing her way and finding it again. Later in this book, I will reveal more about what happened to her after her walk with God began in earnest.

Kate's Story

He stopped by my cubicle and asked me for information. It was a business exchange, but I sensed a warmth in him and was smitten. When he left, I stepped into the aisle and watched as he made his way through the maze of cubicles where we worked. The Cube Farm, we called it—like the Dilbert cartoon, but I wasn't laughing. Not one bit. I was thinking that some day this man would play an important role in my life.

Within a year, I was married to this co-worker I'll call Jonathan. We stayed in Silicon Valley but were transferred to separate work groups. I was brimming with hope. My professional life had been successful and satisfying in many ways; but as a married woman I now felt complete. My career had involved people management, good compensation for hard but interesting work, and lots of travel. Now I needed to feel loved.

It was his second marriage, and two teen sons and a grown daughter came with the package. When people learned about my stepchildren, they would ask: Is this your first marriage? My answer: It's my *only* marriage. And I meant it. To me, it was a forever deal.

Flash forward six years. On a day like any other—both of us commuting to work in our matching company cars—I came home first, turned the key in the lock and stepped into . . . a completely empty house. *We've been robbed!* I thought, charging to the kitchen phone to call police. Even the phone was gone. Chills ran up my spine. I raced to the door, terrified that the burglar was still inside, maybe hiding in a closet. We lived in a gated community. *I'll drive to the security guard. From there I can call . . .*

And that's when I saw it: An envelope propped against the baseboard near the front door. I tore it open. It was a note from Jonathan telling me the marriage was over. No explanation. Certainly no forwarding address. I crumbled in shock and tears.

The next days were a blur. I was an emotional wreck. I had immediate needs, of course, so friends insisted I stay with them. When I say the house was empty, I mean that literally. I did not have a change of clothes. No coffee mug. No toothbrush. He'd left the place move-in ready.

But of all the things he took, what I needed most were the files and records. I could not call our bank or investment firm and say, "I have an account there, but I don't know the number, don't know the password . . ." In other words, I needed help just to find out where I stood financially.

The first lawyer suggested I pawn my wedding rings and come back later with money for his retainer. The second lawyer was more reasonable. He began what was to be a 21-month process that would cost me tens of thousands of dollars and buckets of tears. But it would lead to a wake-up call to reality that created in me a deep dependence on the Lord instead of on myself. I say "dependence" rather than "relationship," because I had committed myself to Christ as a teen and had a walk with the Lord that I considered close. However, it was light years away from what it should have been, as I was to discover in the journey ahead.

Many filings, motions, subpoenas, interrogatories, discovery documents and other legal jargon later, I finally had some information. First, each bank or investment account had a zero balance. Second, my husband had been incarcerated years earlier for white-collar crime.

Well, he was definitely a thief—I could vouch!—and a good one at that. As I went through the mountains of paperwork he was required to produce (after my attorney finally found him), I discovered that Jonathan had actually stolen money from my family on our wedding day. He'd done it by taking a check from my father to reimburse me for wedding expenses (I was an older bride, nearly 40, but my sweet daddy still wanted to pay for "his little girl's" wedding). According to stamps on the back of my dad's check, on our honeymoon, Jonathan converted it to a cashier's check in an apparent effort to end the paper trail. After that he must have deposited it into an account he'd apparently kept in his own name, which was against the agreement we'd made to rename all our accounts jointly. Obviously, this "agreement" (which I'd carried out, not knowing he had not) made it possible for him to remove all my premarital funds plus all we had accumulated during the marriage.

And did I mention that the house was empty? Of course, I did. So by now you get the picture: Every dollar or belonging I had accumulated in my lifetime was gone.

You may think I was so furious that my heart didn't ache. But it did. I had such a torrent of emotions that sorting them out was like separating one raindrop from another. In addition to my broken heart and my (very appropriate) feelings of abandonment, I felt that God had left me. Or, at a minimum, He hadn't prevented this from happening. It was months, perhaps years, before I fully understood that—in His wisdom—He'd allowed this to happen . . . and for my own good.

Through a series of circumstances that only He could orchestrate, I found a solid Bible-believing church with compassionate people who surrounded me with love. Among the lessons I learned: (1) God never left me; (2) God can be trusted; and (3) God was drawing me to a much deeper walk with Him.

I also came to understand that, although I had been taken advantage of, I'd participated in the process through my own sinful nature. You see, although I'd slept with Jonathan only after we were engaged, that's when my instincts about him and even my common sense went out the window. During the complex healing process, I thought back on our courtship and realized that there *were* red flags. But I'd overlooked them, because I was totally invested in him, so to speak. I was blinded by the intensity of inappropriate intimacy, one of many reasons God's perfect plan for His people is to reserve sex for marriage.

The divorce was one of the tiny percentage that ever goes to trial. (Although my assets had vanished, my high-paying job kept a rented roof over my head, provided basic furnishings and clothes; plus it funded my response to the lawsuit.) And in that court of man's law, I learned another lesson: The person with the best attorney wins.

By then, of course, my understanding of "winning" was quite different from what it was earlier in the process. By the time we sat in court, I'd been walking closely with God for nearly two years, a step-by-step journey into an understanding of His divine purposes. I began every day with prayer and Bible study. I guarded my heart carefully by putting on the armor of God as described in Ephesians 6:10-20 (for me, a new kind of "dress for success"). I came to see why being His daughter, even disciplined as such, was more precious than the money or belongings I once treasured.

Surprise, surprise—Jonathan lied in court. The judge fell for it and ordered us to settle. (But, lest you feel sorry for me, consider how many trials Jesus endured and how unjust they were!) I wound up with a fraction of the marital assets (to which I had contributed more than Jonathan by entering the marriage with more money and by earning more in my job). If you don't believe this can happen, please refer back to my conclusion that, in a divorce settlement in the world's justice system, the person with the "best" attorney can come out way, way ahead. I was out-lawyered.

But God's best lesson was still to come. Within weeks, the only asset I received from the settlement suddenly shot up in value. It was a water view lot, and—although I wasn't in the process of trying to sell it—a couple offered me an amount of money that was far above market value. And they had the money to pay for it in one large check.

Suddenly, I went from being a woman with a rental and a few meager furnishings to one who could pay cash for a nice home without even having to get a mortgage. And furnish it to boot!

There's more to this story of God's provision. I had prayed to Him that the water view lot, my one asset from the divorce, eventually would sell for a precise amount of money to accomplish a financial goal. By then, my prayer life was regular, and I had loyal prayer partners. The amount of money was more than 50 percent higher than the lot's value at that time, but I was patient. (To be precise, the focus of my prayer was that I would be able to survive financially without having to sell this high-value asset until it reached the value I needed.) I expected to wait years for the real estate market to grow that much. But God had a plan with much longer-term benefits than financial gain. He brought this couple to me—when the lot wasn't even for sale yet—within weeks of my prayer. With no prompting or knowledge of the amount of money I had prayed to get for the lot, they offered that amount *to the dollar*. And it was to be a cash (by check) transaction.

Don't miss God's message to me, His beloved daughter: Although I was a good earner and had been an astute investor, what He could accomplish on my behalf through miraculous circumstances was far greater than I could possibly accomplish through my own efforts.

I had just the personality to need that kind of spectacular lesson. I was hardheaded, hard-driving and self-sufficient. I needed to know that not only could I trust God, but also that His ways are so much greater than mine that it would be insane to consider taking even the tiniest step without Him.

Now I never do.

For Study

1. Describe a time when you were physically lost.

   Describe a time when you were emotionally lost.

   Describe a time when you were mentally lost.

   Describe a time when you were spiritually lost.

2. Select one of the examples above and describe in detail how you got back to where God wanted you to be before you became lost. Try to break down the process into steps.

3. Consider the steps to finding your way back. On the occasion you described above, you may have found the way on your own. But if you follow Christ as your Savior, the Holy Spirit resides within you to be your guide. Fill in the missing words from this chapter's verse:

   Whether you turn to the right or to the__________, your ears will hear a ______________ behind you, saying, "This is the __________; walk in it" (Isa. 30:21).

Show me the way home, Lord. Direct my steps each and every day, picking me up when I stumble, forgiving me when I fall. Thank You for loving me enough to draw me to You, walking with me on my journey. I pray this in the name of my Savior Jesus. Amen.

4

Praise Renews Hope

Why are you downcast, O my soul? Why so disturbed within me? Put your hope in God, for I will yet praise him, my Savior and my God.
PSALM 43:5

Praise and thankfulness are closely intertwined but are also distinctly different. When I praise someone, I am affirming a truth about who that person *is*. When I thank a person or am thankful for someone, I am affirming a truth about what that person *does*. I don't fully understand why praise has the power to renew hope; I only know that it does.

When we praise God, we are affirming who He is and speaking out loud the qualities that we know are true about Him. Galatians 5:22-23 lists the fruit of the Spirit. The Holy Spirit is a part of the triune God, and whatever qualities He possesses are also the qualities possessed by God Himself and by Jesus, His Son. These verses in Galatians tell us that as we become more like Christ, these nine qualities will be evident in our lives:

- Love
- Joy
- Peace
- Patience
- Kindness
- Goodness
- Faithfulness
- Gentleness
- Self-control

Feeling Hopeless

In 1997, when my husband, Johnny, was diagnosed with stage IV prostate cancer, my hope meter plummeted to rock bottom. For three days I did nothing but cry. We'd received the diagnosis after Johnny had spent an entire day at the hospital having all sorts of scans. We already had the results of his biopsy and knew that six of the seven sites biopsied were malignant. What we didn't know was that the cancer had spread to his bones and his lymph system. "I'm so sorry" were the only words the doctor in the nuclear medicine department could say to us as we left the hospital that night.

We felt hopeless. Johnny had not eaten all day, and he was starving. I was a wreck and couldn't stop crying. He assured me that I would be all right and even gave me his sunglasses to wear as we entered the Mexican restaurant. I must have looked really weird, since it was October, and at 6:30 in the evening it was already dark! We went to the back of the restaurant, and I sat facing the corner so I wouldn't look too obvious wearing the dark glasses. I'm sure that as I stifled sobs and my shoulders heaved, the waitress must have thought my husband was a wife beater and I was hiding a black eye. I can report that I was able to eat all of my dinner!

By then we had bought the little cottage that looked out on Galveston Bay. That night we drove down there, because our home in Houston was not empty. Our son, John, and his wife, Lisa, and their three children had been there since Thursday of the previous week when their home burned to the ground. (Yes, more family tragedy!) Because we knew the news from the doctor probably wasn't going to be good, we told the kids we'd spend the night at the bay.

I'm so glad we made that decision, because I did nothing but cry for the next three days. I felt terrible that Johnny was the one with the cancer and all he could do was try to comfort me. After three days, I confessed to Johnny how sorry I was that I couldn't be strong for him. I'll never forget what he said to me that morning: "How do you think I would feel if you were strong right now?" I was able to laugh when he said that because it was actually a comfort to him that I was as devastated as he was, and it gave him something to focus on: trying to make me feel better.

Peace at Last

I wish I could say that we prayed the minute we left the hospital, but we didn't. Sometimes when our hopes are dashed, prayer is the last thing we think to do. Peace finally came to us when we crawled up in the middle of our bed that night and simply praised God together for who He is. When we finally turned to God, we were still too hurt and confused to formulate a sensible list of our requests. I'm sure we asked for help, but it was vague. We were too muddled to detail a list of petitions. So we simply praised Him. We told Him we believed in His goodness and wisdom and would follow Him down this path. We gave Him our hearts, raw but trusting. It was not the sort of joyful praise you may picture, but looking back, I realize it was a form of praise nonetheless. It was all we could manage, but God used it for good.

I tell you this story because Johnny's cancer diagnosis was the beginning of my learning the power of praise.

We settled into a routine after the initial diagnosis and, by the way, never went back home. Son John and his family lived in our Houston house for almost two years while they rebuilt theirs. We realized that God had divinely orchestrated everything perfectly for all of us during this horrible time. John and Lisa had lived less than a mile from us, so their children could still catch the same bus every morning for school. Being in our home gave their lives a semblance of order as they rebuilt their home. God provided for their every need much like He has provided for ours since Hurricane Ike. They were able to live in a home that was totally furnished, just like we've been doing.

Johnny and I rocked along the next year, getting used to the fact that he had cancer. We went to a lodge in Colorado Springs and went through a detox program together, a cleansing that used an all-raw diet that we continued for six months. During that time his PSA increased from 48 to 65, so we began researching other medical options. We went for a consult at a leading cancer hospital in Houston. After spending the entire day there we were told by the doctor that there was nothing they could do except continuous hormone therapy. The doctor said that after a couple of years,

Johnny's body would become resistant to the hormones, and they wouldn't work any longer.

I'll never forget Johnny asking the doctor, "Are you saying that I only have a couple of years to live?" The doctor replied, "I think I made myself perfectly clear." Well, we left that hospital with our hopes dashed but just enough anger to start doing our homework. I read everything that I could get my hands on about prostate cancer.

Enter Dr. Leibowitz

During this time, someone in First Place 4 Health sent us a videotape of a doctor in California, who was presenting his views on the treatment of prostate cancer. The next time we went to our urologist for Johnny's hormone shot we asked our doctor about Dr. Leibowitz's theory and treatment. The doctor said, "Why would you want to do that?" Long story short, we went to Los Angeles for a consultation with Dr. Bob Leibowitz, and after 13 months of hormone therapy we left his office that day full of hope that Dr. Bob would be able to extend Johnny's life.

I took a week's vacation just a year after Johnny's cancer diagnosis. That week, as I was having my quiet time, I had an astounding revelation. I realized that I'd checked out emotionally from my work and my staff during the past year. Keep in mind that I still went to work, traveled and spoke during this time, but I'd not been there emotionally. I realized that God had actually been carrying me for an entire year.

When I returned to work, I shared with our staff what I'd learned that vacation week. They looked at me and smiled because they already knew that God had been carrying me, and they had been carrying me as well. After one of the most miserable years of my life, I had learned the power of praise.

I had so many things to praise God for. I praised Him that He is sovereign. He knows everything; and because I am His child, He loves me. He was there those three days when I couldn't stop crying, but He knew I needed time to grieve. As soon as we had the sense to stop crying long enough to praise Him, God's peace came to us, and it never left.

I praised Him because He is the God who provides. God knew what was going to happen, and He led Johnny to experience an urgency to buy a little place at the bay. So we had this haven where we could retreat and grieve together. Then God provided our doctor in Los Angeles, and we still go there today after 12 years. (Yes, that's right—a dozen years after the previous doctor "made himself perfectly clear" that Johnny had only two years to live, he has survived.) Our doctor works with another oncologist here in Houston so that we only go to California every few months.

Because God is sovereign and He also provides, we knew that He would pick the absolutely best publisher for our First Place 4 Health program, and the company happens to be located in Ventura, California, just an hour north of Los Angeles. The owners of Gospel Light, Bill and Rhonni Greig, have become dear friends, and we always stay in their home when we fly out to see the doctor. During those visits, I have editorial meetings, and Johnny can eat all the sushi he wants for a couple of days.

It's no coincidence that we first visited Dr. Leibowitz in Los Angeles in June 1999, and by the summer of 2000, God had provided a new publisher located an hour away from our doctor. What could have been a difficult trip has become sweet beyond words. Our God is also the God who sees. He sees what we need, and He works it all out perfectly.

So, if our God knows everything, sees everything and provides for everything we need, is He not worthy of our praise?

Praising the God Who Changes Us

We praise God because He is worthy of our praise. But there's another reason to learn the power of praise. You see, praising God for who He is changes who we are. We begin to see that our problems are not problems. God is bigger than our problems, and He is able to help in our time of greatest need. We go from hopeless to hope-filled.

I've heard people say that they feel so spiritually bankrupt that "praising God is *all* I can do." It saddens me that some consider the act of praising God inferior to other forms of approaching our heavenly Father, because that's simply not true. I wonder if the notion of praise as a prelude to prayer springs from a four-part list many of us learned as a framework for our prayer time:

1. Praise God for who He is.
2. Thank Him for blessing you, naming the ways.
3. Confess your sins to Him.
4. Ask for His help, guidance and provisions.

People who are in the habit of praying to God every morning may use this format. It can be a once-every-24-hour opportunity to review the events of the previous day, big and small (Lord, thank You for the good report I got from the doctor yesterday . . . thank You for the comfort of my faithful dog . . . please forgive me for not holding my tongue when yesterday's meeting dissolved into a gripe session) and to look forward to the upcoming day, petitioning His help (Lord, watch over me as I fly to Birmingham . . . be with Colleen as she begins a new job). They also may speak to God at other times during the day—perhaps the burst of an "arrow prayer" at a critical moment. Yet I wonder if, by using this four-part format, some may think of beginning with praise as the simple part of the process, their way of easing into daily prayer time like an opera singer might warm up his throat by singing a scale.

Forgive me if I'm stepping on your toes. I encourage people to use a format like this, especially daily! But if you do, know that praising God is not the warm-up act before the top-billing performer comes on stage. It's just as essential as the other three parts of the list.

Praising God is important, worthwhile and necessary. God wants our praise, not because He needs applause but because He wants us to fully appreciate and focus on His greatness for our own good and our development as believers. In the Old Testament book of Job, chapters 38 through 41, the Lord speaks directly to Job with details of His vast creation and descriptions of His grandeur. God is saying to Job that He is bigger and more complex than Job and his friends can perceive. God's message to Job is that, by knowing of His greatness, Job will realize that He is trustworthy. Job will continue to be "blameless and upright, a man who fears God and shuns evil," as we learn in Job 1:8, which is the Lord's own description of His righteous servant. You see, Job, at one point in his pain and sorrow, even considered ending his own life; but now he would know that God could be trusted to bring his misery to an end. As Christians, we know the rest of the story because we have the facts in the New Testament. Because of Jesus' suffering, death and resurrection, we too can have redemption, restoration and rebirth. This is hope!

A dear friend who wrote in an email about the business she and her husband own said that despite the toll it has taken on them to drain their personal investments and savings to cover their payroll and taxes, she knows "this low point is where the Lord meets me and trains me to walk with Him, one day at a time and focused on the next right thing; because it is when I look too far ahead that I feel the most hopeless." She went on to say, "regardless of being tired, sad and often lonely, I know that good will be worked out in our lives for God's glory. This is the place where we trust and obey." In their marriage, she and her husband deliberately praise God in tough circumstances, because it's an essential part of the process that leads to holiness.

By the way, Johnny has had stage IV cancer for 12 years, so every day we have together is a sweet gift from God that we don't take for granted. He gifted us with our fiftieth wedding anniversary in June 2009, something we never would have dreamed possible at the time of his diagnosis in 1997. And did I mention that Johnny's PSA levels have decreased? We praise God mightily for that!

The Power of Praise

Praising God is essential to living a hope-filled life, and praise has the power to change our relationships on earth as well. Genuine praise of other people will change them and change us too.

Praise is one of the methods God uses to heal a dismal marriage. If you are struggling in your marriage, why not try this? List 20 admirable attributes of your husband. Remember, this is who he is, not what he does. Is he honest, hard working, helpful, a good dad? Husband, do the same for your wife. Is she committed, resourceful, fun, a good mom? After doing this exercise, watch how God uses it to change your heart—and, hopefully, your behavior—when you try step two in the process, which is to praise your spouse for these attributes. As you do this, it will become easier and easier.

Recently, a friend shared that she and her husband fight every year when they put up the outdoor Christmas lights. She said her husband doesn't do it right and gets angry when she tries to give him advice on how to do it better. This year, she asked him, "How can I help?" He replied, "Stay inside the house." (What she really wondered was what she could *do*. "Should I just duck under the strand that's hanging in front of the doorway?") I was thinking about our conversation and realized that praise, in this instance, could have a powerful effect on their marriage: "You always do such a good job with this, honey. I'll just go inside and work on another project."

Her husband is a wonderful dad, and he keeps the children each morning so his wife can exercise; plus he helps them get ready for school. Where criticism has the power to make us feel worthless, praise builds up and heals. If this young mom can learn the power of genuine, honest praise, it will revitalize and energize her marriage. All of us need praise for who we are; and every person who knows Christ has some essential qualities that are deserving of praise. Review the list of qualities in Galatians 5:22-23, known as fruit of the Spirit, and see if some or all of those qualities apply.

Praise renews hope. I don't know why this is true, but I have learned it through the trials I have gone through and am certain that it never fails.

You might be having a problem with one of your children. Why not try making a list of everything you love about this child. Remember, your list will be about *who they are*, not what they do.

Is this child essentially loving, gentle, sensitive, kind? Find ways to genuinely praise your offspring—whether children or grown adults—for the qualities you see in them. It won't happen overnight, but you will begin to see positive change, not only in you but also in them.

Praise is also powerful in the workplace. When you have a problem with a co-worker, take time to write down attributes you admire in the person. She might be friendly—maybe so friendly that she never stays at her desk and doesn't get her work done. Nevertheless, her friendliness is part of who she is. Find a way to praise her for this quality and you will see changes in your own feelings as well.

Another co-worker might be just the opposite. Not only is he not friendly, he might be hostile and negative. What can you list as a positive attribute? Is he loyal? Does he have a good work ethic? Look for ways to genuinely praise this person and eventually the walls of hurt will begin to come down.

Because you are giving praise for who they are, not what they do, they will realize that you genuinely care about them. Praising others is something that will grow in us as we practice doing it. It isn't easy to love someone who is unlovable. When I am around someone like this, I ask God to love this person through me. I am always amazed when I end up loving someone I could hardly stand to be around before I began finding ways to praise her.

Yes, praise renews hope. When it does, we realize how important it is to praise God and to praise people and circumstances in our life. We can begin this discipline by praising God when our heart is so confused and broken that praise is the only kind of prayer we can offer. And yet, He honors it, and then that method of reaching out becomes part of who we are.

More Real-life Stories

This story involves two friends of mine—a married couple. Our relationship goes back to childhood—attending camp together. Joan has played the piano at our church for more than 50 years. I learned that Joan was in the ICU, unresponsive, and with an undiagnosed problem (later diagnosed as West Nile Virus, from which she recovered). It was scary. One day I received an email from an ICU nurse who happens to be in my First Place 4 Health class. (Isn't it wonderful to be members of the family of God with all these connections?!) Because of patient confidentiality, I'll stick to first names.

Joan and John's Story

Joan's nurse wrote: "I am so excited and just want God to get the praise. Friday, I took care of Joan, and when I went in she started mumbling a few words. Then an hour or so later the doctor came in, and John was there. She said a few more words and was following commands like moving her hands and legs when we asked her to. Then John went to a meeting and said he would return later.

"As I worked with her, she started waking up and began talking and moving everything. When John returned, Joan was just talking and joking and having a great time. We were all praising the Lord in her room, and the whole floor wondered what was going on. No one could believe it—none of the nurses or the team of doctors on her case. It was a miracle!

"That afternoon we sat her in a chair. John gave her a keyboard and she began playing it. She's still weak and a little confused about time and does not remember being 'out of it,' but she praises God for the victory. She was a bit hesitant playing the keyboard, but one of the songs was so appropriate: 'Praise God from whom all blessings flow.' "

Another story comes through my good friend Jaye Martin, a gifted author and speaker who develops women in leadership positions. A doctoral candidate at Southern Baptist Theological Seminary, Jaye is a wonderful example of how praise will bring out the best in potential leaders and help them find their true giftedness. The following is adapted from her latest book *Women Leading*

Women: The Biblical Model for the Church.[1] This vignette was written by her co-author, Terri Stovall.

"Suzanne"

Suzanne was always the first to volunteer. She wanted to be a part of everything. Her enthusiastic attitude would help us overlook the rough edges and awkwardness that made finding a permanent place of service difficult. When I mentioned in passing that I was looking for a new Sunday School teacher, she immediately volunteered, but that was not really the place for her. She was involved in some way with every committee that helped plan the retreat. Some of that interaction with people went well; other people chalked it up to, "Well, that's just Suzanne." I soon found myself with the attitude of just putting up with Suzanne and giving her things to do to placate her.

One day, Suzanne stopped by my office. Her exuberance was not quite there that day. In fact, she was as solemn as I had ever seen her. When we sat down together, she took a deep breath and told me through tear-filled eyes that she loved her church and just wanted to find something she could do. She wanted to find her place. We talked a long time, and for the first time, I saw Suzanne as the woman God created her to be. A woman who loved Jesus, she was growing in Him and was willing to give everything she had to be used by Him.

Over the next months, I worked with Suzanne individually. We spent time looking at spiritual gifts and the responsibility of using those gifts. We talked through the different skills she had, and I helped her realize that even those things that seemed to be everyday abilities for her were skills that could be used in the church. The most meaningful time spent was talking through her life experiences and how God could use those experiences for others. It was touching to see a woman talk about the hard road she had walked and the differences with which she lived. She grew in the process to realize that these things were not deficiencies but weaknesses through which God could work.

Then we began to try different places of service. We tried all kinds of things, but nothing seemed just right. Watching her, I began to see a trend. Her favorite thing to do was to talk to people, give them a smile and always say something positive. I soon came up with an idea. Suzanne became our official women's Bible study greeter. It was her job to be at the women's Bible study 15 minutes early and to make sure everyone who came was greeted with a smile and a positive word of encouragement.

Suzanne thrived in that role. It gave her a sense of purpose. The women in the Bible study began to see Suzanne as an important part of the Bible study experience. On the rare occasion when she was absent, she was sorely missed, and many of the women made sure Suzanne knew that. Today Suzanne is a different person. She still has her unique differences, but she has matured and grown through this place of service as only Suzanne can. Everyone has a place of service in God's kingdom.

For Study

1. List specific ways you can begin using praise in your life. Include ways to use praise by your actions as well as your words.

   In the list below, write praiseworthy attributes about each one:

   God

   Spouse

   Child, grandchild or relative

   Friend

Boss, employee or co-worker

____

____

____

____

2. Pick at least one person from the list above and describe how praise of that person will change *you*, your attitude, your circumstances.

____

____

____

____

____

____

I praise You, my Lord and Savior, for being my guiding light, for being my beacon of hope. I praise You for being faithful in all Your promises. I praise You for loving me, even when I am not lovable. Amen.

5

Prayer Revives Hope

Be joyful in hope, patient in affliction, faithful in prayer.
ROMANS 12:12

On the day I'm writing this chapter, the news is full of trash . . . literally.

I'm not kidding.

A volcano has erupted in Iceland, sending ash into the atmosphere, interfering with air travel for days, maybe weeks. Tons of plastic are swirling in mid-Atlantic Ocean currents near the Azores islands. And a movie debuts today with a title that seems even coarser than our culture has become, if that's possible. Okay, technically the offending word in the film's title is found in the Bible, but it's used in a different way.

I promise you I'm not a prude, and the point of this chapter will not be to lecture readers about language. I'm simply making the contrast between the world's reality and God's perfect will for us, which is to be holy.

"Holy." What does that word mean to you? Does it conjure images of golden halos over the heads of biblical figures dressed in colorful garments? Or do you have the more realistic view of holiness . . . and how we can achieve it through prayer?

A Culture of Coarseness

In the beginning of the chapter I mentioned three items in today's news. Let's unpack and analyze them from the vastly contrasting perspectives of today's culture of coarseness and the holiness that Christ-followers seek.

A Volcano Erupts in Iceland

Thousands of airline flights are cancelled due to decreased visibility and microscopic debris that can be sucked into airplane engines, shutting them down. Today is the biggest disruption of air travel since the terrorist attacks we call "9/11."

This volcano is the latest in a spate of natural disasters—earthquakes, hurricanes, tsunamis. The event will cause believers to pray, asking God to watch over travelers and others affected by the volcano that is spewing gigantic clouds of ash. It will cause some people to question God (which I say is fine, if they must—at least they're thinking of Him and considering His powers). Still others (and here I'm imagining towers full of frustrated air traffic controllers) may curse Him.

I can't know for sure what God thinks of that, but I have my suspicions that He's happier to have them acknowledging His authority over every aspect of life on earth and elsewhere than to have them ignoring Him; I know that He yearns to connect with all of us. Sadly, some people who are cursing Him are doing so out of ignorance—like the volcano, they are blowing off steam rather than engaging with the Creator of the universe who has a reason for everything, including natural events based on His perfect plan.

Trash in the Ocean

The second news item is about a sprawling patch of confetti-like plastic floating in the ocean. Vast clumps of garbage like this have been discovered before, the results of our throwaway culture that uses disposable products that are not biodegradable.

Although we have traveled to the moon and back, we have not developed a way to clean the world's oceans. Man's footprints were left on the lunar surface, probably not a concern, but now man's debris is collecting into enormous swirls controlled by water currents.

Okay, along with no lectures about coarse language, I promise no lectures about our lack of care for God's creation, known in some circles as environmentalism. My comment here is that

I'm not surprised. The image of garbage littering hundreds of miles of ocean, much of it visible at the surface, is consistent with the coarseness I see in our culture.

A New Movie Release

News item number three is the opening of a movie that I know little about except for its title. It might be hugely entertaining, maybe even more innocent than its name implies (but I doubt it). My point is that it uses a word that—until recently—no news outlet would print, even in the movies section.

Remember that I'm from the era when the Easter morning headline in our local newspaper stated: "He Is Risen." I'm not pining for the "good ol' days," because all days have their problems (a biblical fact, by the way). But I am commenting on a culture that is far from holy.

Seeking Holiness Through Prayer

Prayer is our most effective weapon against being suffocated by the debris around us and within us, and by our own self-absorption. Prayer turns our face and focus away from what is temporal, profane and common (in the older sense of the word "common," as in not being dedicated to the sacred).

Prayer will lift us up and out. Prayer is our lifeline. Prayer is our direct communication with the God of the universe . . . and He is willing and *eager* to connect with us.

Choosing to pray is a choice to grow close to the One who loves us far beyond our capacity to even *comprehend* love. Taking time to pray regularly initiates communication with the One who *always wants to listen* . . . and to tell us the Truth. Praying is an act of submission to the One who will deliver *in perfection* the intimacy we crave.

Prayer is the pathway for a holy walk; holiness is the opposite of corruption. I find that maintaining an attitude of prayerfulness, a continuous connection to God in my soul, creates a barrier between my heart and the overwhelming coarseness of the world. Prayer is the very process by which that coarseness *in us* is transformed from our original fallen state to our potential for purity and holiness. Prayer also focuses our sights like a laser on God, saving us from our egocentric—and deadly—view of reality.

Holiness is related to excellent health. Madeleine L'Engle wrote, "It is no coincidence that the root word of *whole, health, heal, holy* is *hale* (as in *hale* and *hearty*). If we are healed, we become whole . . . we are holy."[1]

Ah, the power of His unrelenting love.

Praying changes us. Because of free will, we can choose to be troubled by the "stuff" of this world or we can seek holiness, which is available to us. Prayer can draw us back from the abyss of destruction; it can create in us gushing and inexplicable joy or it can simply soothe our weary heart.

Break me, Lord, until I'm wholly Yours. This may be our holiest plea to the Lord, because in this prayer, we are asking—begging—to become His. We are inviting Him to break us, like a wrangler breaks a wild stallion. We are urging Him to take our self-will and remake it into His will.

We are submitting . . . wholly. Our prayer is to become . . . holy.

Real-life Story

Prayers have enormous influence over the forces of evil. Read about a woman whose adoptive parents were tremendous prayer warriors for her, a legacy they passed along and which she uses today as a parent and grandparent. Her life was spared and her circumstances improved on so many levels that it will take your breath away.

Prayer Gives Hope

By Lancia E. Smith

I am unequivocally the product of prayer: specifically, my parents' prayers and those of their friends. If it were not for their faithful prayers during my decades of wrong turns, bad choices and other fallout from a childhood marked by tragedy and abuse, I would not be alive today and certainly would not have become the person I am.

Today I understand this concept even more deeply. I see that my parents co-labored with God by praying over me as their ongoing role in His loving process of my redemption.

First some background. In 1969, my parents, who had been unable to have children naturally, became willing to take in a foster child at the prompting of friends. Through a series of conversations at church, they found that another couple had a 15-year-old female foster child—me—who was living with them and needed permanent placement. Meetings followed, qualifications were explored and decisions were made step by step. Through each phase, my soon-to-be parents, and close friends in their home group, prayed for God's will to be accomplished.

I met them for the first time in September 1970. I loved Suzanne from the minute I saw her, and we had an immediate connection. She eventually became Mom. I was uncertain about Scott, but at least I was not terrified of him. Given what I'd experienced in my past, my trepidation toward males was inevitable and not a reflection in any way on this man I came to love and call Dad.

I had been in four foster homes over that past summer. I'd been orphaned at age 12-and-a-half and adopted. Then about two years later I became a ward of the state when the original adoptive family was required to relinquish the adoption. My childhood prior to my birth mother's death had been full of abuse, neglect and trauma. Unfortunately, the first adoptive family contributed additional abuse, and authorities intervened.

Ironically, that summer had not been all bad. While attending youth group I had joyfully come to know Christ after hearing the gospel for the first time. I was filled with all the passion and enthusiasm of a new believer.

However, I was like an iceberg—massive needs and brokenness lying beneath the surface, out of sight. The courts and child psychologists had offered their professional opinions. Most were not optimistic, and some who spoke about me were outright grim. I remember hearing several people say they did not expect me to survive to age 20 because of the types of trauma I'd experienced—multiple perpetrators since infancy, continuing patterns of repetitive abuses. Looking back, I realize that, by the time of this adoption, I was a fragile young teen who had not been protected by the adults in my life. As a result, there was little hope for my extended future. Yet, with solemn reservations, God gave Scott and Suzanne a green light to take me and, covered in much prayer, I moved into their home on October 31, 1970, just into my sophomore year in high school.

They surrounded me with love, stability, direction, kindness—in short, godliness—for the next three years that I lived with them. Despite the inevitable episodes of crisis, I remember those years as some of the happiest of my life because of their love. The beauty of living in their God-filled and orderly home was beyond anything I had experienced, and the deep rhythm of living God's way was planted in me, although it would be a long time before I could actually duplicate the same kind of life on my own.

It wasn't long though before the dark underbelly of the iceberg began to surface. Among other problems, I continued to battle acute depressive episodes, and during one, I tried alcohol, thinking it would provide an escape into sleep. Instead, it produced an extreme, semi-psychotic reaction, including hallucinations and a blackout. That single episode of drinking in high school exposed a terrible biochemical weakness in me—a foreshadowing of events yet to happen. The experience was so terrifying that I did not take another drink for five years.

My parents' prayers, and the prayers of others concerned for me, carried me through the upheaval of those years—years of depression, disassociation, grappling for identity, dealing with staggering losses, suicide attempts, growing in faith and knowledge of God, and trying to figure out how to relate to people. My parents seemed tireless in their prayers. Their focus was not merely on the enormous damage done to me, but also the infinitely greater character and capacity of God. Their prayers for me remain much the same, even to this day.

Despite their earnest appeals to stay with them after high school, and even an amazingly generous offer from my mom's father to pay for college, I could not accept the offers. My shame was so deep.

To their disappointment, I married the day after graduation from high school in a lost girl's effort to establish her own lasting family. Much to my joy, less than a year later, I gave birth to my first child, a beautiful daughter we named Regina. Six months later my husband and I moved to Dallas.

For a brief while, it must have seemed like the end for my parents—all the love and teaching they had provided in such a fleeting time. But the Lord would not so easily release them from their prayer "burdens."

Miraculously, despite my brevity of time in their home and my profound emotional damage, my parents and I had formed a real and lasting bond. I called them while living away and came back to visit over the holidays. Even though I'd only spent three years with them, by the time I struck out on my own as a married woman, my parents were truly my anchor and home. I was drawn to them like shattered metal to a magnet, most likely a result of their strong and relentless prayers for me.

Plus, the brutal reality was that I had nowhere else to go for home and no one else to identify with as family. The legal system separated me from my sisters, and my extended family of origin made no attempt to contact me, although they lived in the same small city. My name was changed as part of the adoption; every picture I had of my family of origin was taken away and destroyed; every piece of familiar furniture sold and removed. Essentially, I was thrown away as well. (An attorney friend tells me that we are still read as a case study by the leading law school in Colorado.)

Meanwhile, God was using these devastating experiences of my childhood and adolescence for a greater good in my life than I possibly could comprehend at that time. I believe His purposes were beyond my parents' abilities to understand as well. However, their faith in God's character to redeem His children exceeded their comprehension, so faith always formed the basis for their actions. One of the crucial lessons I eventually learned from their example is that I can trust God to care for my loved ones even when I cannot. Of course, I didn't understand that truth at the time.

In fact, my emotional issues were getting worse in the midst of isolation in Texas. I had a miscarriage a year and a half after Regina's birth. That loss has lingered with me since. A year after that I gave birth to my son, Daniel. He was a large baby but deceptively frail. The pregnancy and birth were difficult, and I had been confined to bed rest for three months.

After his birth, I descended into a severe postpartum depression. Combined with the isolation, depression and months of failed counseling, my marriage finally crumbled six months after Daniel's arrival. I was absolutely overwhelmed with confusion, pain, loss and a responsibility load beyond my abilities to meet. I was a 22-year-old going on 12 or younger emotionally. Returning to my parents' home on the pretext of showing them the baby, I desperately needed some space to gain perspective, and I also needed to feel secure somewhere. I secretly hoped that my absence would trigger a desire on the part of my husband to reunite, but sadly, it did not.

Going out socially one night proved ruinous for me. The five years of no drinking had not suspended my pathological reaction to alcohol.

Within six weeks I was drinking a quart of vodka a day. I essentially walked off a cliff mentally. It is a miracle that I survived what followed in my life. The fact that we survived the heartache of those times—what Dad refers to as "the difficult years"—is also a testimony to God's unrelenting power to redeem coupled with my parents' faithful and persistent prayers. Despite all appearances of my being lost, my parents did not let go of God's Word or His promises.

Alcoholism and drug addiction consumed me for the next six-and-a-half years. It resulted in my giving the care of Regina and Daniel first to my parents and eventually conceding custody to my former husband and his new wife. I lived on the street, homeless, for a while. I lost all my possessions, my family, my identity . . . and my mind. This was the lowest point of my life, worse even than my childhood, and I still think of it with great sadness.

Astonishingly, I did not lose my faith in God; and though I couldn't form any semblance of an obedient walk with Him, He never let go of His hold on me. As dreadful as those times were, I am deeply and humbly aware that I also was protected from many horrible things that could have befallen me in the places I frequented, and yet I was spared. I am certain this was a direct result of the prayers of others for me, even in my fallen condition.

While I was a practicing addict, I remarried into a far more destructive relationship than my first marriage; and from that point my life plunged into complete insanity. Yet out of that marriage three good things came: the birth of my daughter, Pahtyana; repentance that was true and soul-deep; and, eventually, lasting recovery from addiction. But the marriage, and the terror of it, lasted eight-and-a-half years.

Pahtyana was born in 1980. My repentance experience is directly connected to her birth and the circumstances surrounding it. This was nearly 10 years after my parents and I first met, and they had been praying for me through trauma, heartache, sin and setbacks ever since.

My repentance was the true turning point. It was the seed of life in me, which they had been praying for all those years. It would be an additional two years before I would enter into full recovery with Alcoholics Anonymous, but the beginning of change came at this point. My enemy still had some power, but his hold on me was broken. He won a few battles, but my God won the war. I am certain this only took place because of the decade of prayers by my parents and their many fellow believers who labored over me before the Lord.

It bears saying here that one of the most important things my parents ever did for me (and there were so many) is this: When, after all their best efforts, I chose to remain in darkness, they let me go and trusted God for the outcome. I cannot imagine the pain and struggle it must have caused them to release me; but trust Him they did, and enable my sin they did not. Their deep, abiding, tough and true love was absolutely crucial to my making the choice later to choose life.

When I repented of all the sin, and the minefield of damage I had created by age 25, I changed permanently. There never was any going back. I joined AA and never had another drink, drug or cigarette again. This is important, because my parents did not stay enmeshed with me during this period—it was their time of letting go. Because I misunderstood this ultimately loving decision on their part, I was very hurt and very angry about it for a long, long time.

Even though my parents and I didn't speak for several years, the Lord knew that our relationship would survive and one day even thrive. God led them the right way, for their sakes and ultimately for mine. Their adherence to what was right rather than trying to accommodate me made real and lasting change possible. They chose life, and by their actions put that same choice before me.

I cannot adequately express how deep a debt I owe them for this. The separation between us, which occurred during that period, God later restored to the original sweetness we first had together, and then to something so much richer in the past five years (nearly 35 years later). Today it's as though I were their natural-born child, and we'd always been intertwined. Truly God has done something in each of us that defies all of our expectations!

During the worst years of my early twenties, when things looked so hopeless for me, the Lord told my mother that I would have a happy end—I would be happy in my forties and would be well. At that time in my development, I didn't believe I would live beyond my twenties, or at most maybe early thirties. That assurance from God to my mother became the most powerful agent against my demons, because she believed it and I believed it. It carried the power of God's Word in a way that was living and effective. She and my dad prayed in faith accordingly.

I received that knowledge in the depth of my soul even while I walked in sin as an addict. Their prayers carried me through a second divorce; 10 years of being a single mother in recovery; years of struggling, financially and emotionally, to regain stability; and my going to college as an adult student.

In 1991, I was growing deeper in my walk with the Lord, had become part of a community of believers while teaching in the private Christian school that Pahtyana attended, was gaining ground in recovery, was experiencing some stability as a single mother, was enjoying great success as a student, and was just beginning to pick up the pieces from the death of my significant other a year earlier. My two children from my first marriage, Regina and Daniel, were spending summers and Christmas with me;

those were joyous times. I also was making preparations to move to England in January for a semester abroad for work on my honor's thesis.

On a sunny Friday afternoon in October, I received the phone call every parent dreads. Daniel, 15, and asthmatic, yet cleared for sports by his doctor, had gone out for cross-country track team that fall. During the last race of their season, he suffered an acute asthma attack and, despite everyone's best efforts, went into a coma before paramedics could reach him.

Through the extraordinary efforts of our friends to get immediate plane tickets so we could travel from Colorado to Wisconsin, we were able to reach him while he was still alive. Prayers were lifted for Daniel and for all of us by hundreds of believers on different prayer chains across the country. Those prayers created an invisible cushion that would surround us through the immediate days of his death and in the long years of healing that have followed. Like Sheldon Vanauken's extraordinary work of the same name, we were met with "a severe mercy."

My time with my son at his bedside was overwhelmingly surreal. Daniel was six feet tall at 15 years of age, and his feet nearly hung over the end of the bed at Children's Hospital in Milwaukee where he had been flown on a Flight to Life helicopter. He looked so perfect—no outward appearances indicated how broken were his internal systems. Already on life support when I got there, tubes in his nose draining oxygenated blood out of his stomach, he simply looked like he was sleeping. His mouth moved like it did when he was a baby nursing, and for several hours tears drained out of his eyes from the outside corners and trailed down his cheeks.

I held his hand—his beautiful, long fingers lay still in mine—and then I said, "I love you, Daniel, with all of my heart and soul. I am so sorry for all the things I failed to do for you as your mother." I was crying. At that moment he gave my fingers the tiniest squeeze! I knew then that he was aware I was there and could hear me. It was a gesture that has resonated with me ever since, both as Daniel's connection to me and as a gift from God in the midst of my life's most agonizing moments. Then, powerless to change or prevent it, my beloved only son slipped quietly into the arms of God that night and, like everyone who has lost a child will tell you, part of me died with him.

The expression of God's mercy that has carried perhaps the most lingering effect remarkably came through Daniel's own words. A story he wrote in eighth grade called "The Race" was given to Daniel's father by his teacher. Daniel—gifted, brilliant and humble boy that he was—never mentioned it, nor that he had won an award for it.

In the story, Daniel described a runner in a long-distance race across changing terrain. At first it is smooth, with a racecourse only wide enough for a single runner. As he runs, the terrain changes and becomes more difficult. He runs up over a hill and—focusing on his path ahead—he sees another runner, a competitor. The other runner, dressed in black, is neither human nor friendly. Daniel's protagonist is attacked by this creature (a demon), then rescued by another runner. Now Daniel's fictional runner and his rescuer run together for a time. Eventually, they are separated by a divided path. The main character faces many challenges and difficulties after this and is aided in several ways.

Nearing the end of the race, he struggles desperately to make it to the finish line before the sun sets. Suddenly, he is beset with a terrible cramp that cripples him in pain as he gasps for breath. Darkness sets in, and he knows he is going to die. Then Daniel wrote: "He stumbled. Fell. Was caught . . ." The runner had fallen into the arms of the King who had been his rescuer earlier! "They walked together into paradise and talked . . ." Those words, prophetically written by my son, have consoled and informed me through years of overwhelming pain. Whenever I feel at the edge of sanity and about to slip off into the abyss, I am reminded by Jesus that Daniel fell directly into the Savior's arms that day and is now waiting safely for us and happily with Him at home.

Redemption is not without cost or pain, either for us or for God. But there is a deep, sobering consolation in knowing that God suffered with us then, suffers with us still and someday will wipe away every tear. I rest my hope on His Word about that.

The Lord's word to my mother years earlier came to pass. Throughout everything that happened, I stayed sober. To date I am 28 years and counting free of all alcohol, drugs and cigarettes! Over the years I sponsored numerous women in AA, did lay counseling and support work with other battered women, plus rape and childhood sexual abuse survivors, led recovery groups in churches, served on boards and service organizations, worked in bereavement groups and spoke to groups about God's power and faithfulness.

In 1994, after 10 years of being a single mother, I met my husband, Peter. We married a year later, and I "inherited" his three beautiful children. My parents prayed faithfully for our new blended family to bond as a loving, cohesive and Christ-reflecting unit. What a glory to God to be able to say we remain happily married after 15 years, and our children have all thrived.

The hope I have seen renewed and sustained in my parents because of their prayers is the hope I cling to in praying for my own children. God is faithful! One of my favorite Scripture verses is Psalm 42:5: "Why are you downcast, O my soul? Why so disturbed within me? Put your hope in God, for I will yet praise him, my Savior and my God." He knows the longings of our heart and delights to fulfill them. He does hear and answer our prayers.

For Study

1. Do you believe that God can be influenced by our prayers? Read the following passages in the Bible. Jot notes about what's recorded for us in Scripture about God hearing the prayers, cries and pleas of His people.

   Genesis 6:1-8

   Exodus 32:9-14

   2 Kings 20:1-6

   2 Chronicles 32:24-26

   Psalm 106:43-45

   Jeremiah 18:5-8

Jonah 3:5-10

2. Read Matthew 26:36-46 in which Jesus prays in the Garden of Gethsemane, asking His Father to let the cup be taken from Him. Would there have been a point to this prayer if Jesus did not have a fundamental belief that prayers can cause change—sometimes? Write your understanding of this passage.

3. Because God is the perfect Father and knows what is best for us, He does not always grant the wishes (prayers) of His children. Make notations here about a prayer you have prayed and, looking back, why you believe God did or did not answer it.

Heavenly Father, thank You for Your perfect wisdom and will for my life. Thank You for always being available to me, for listening to my heart and for providing what is best. Thank You for lifting me out of the coarseness of the world and sheltering me from the debris, even within myself. Thank You for leading me to holiness. Amen.

6

Forgiveness Restores Hope

For if you forgive men when they sin against you,
your heavenly Father will also forgive you.
MATTHEW 6:14

Ah, Shari. My precious daughter killed by a drunk driver.

Losing a child before you leave this earth is a parent's worst nightmare. I cannot speak for mothers and fathers who have experienced this devastating loss through means such as terminal illness, where the passing may be slow but inevitable—full of hope and promise one day, heartbreak the next. Perhaps in those cases there is time for good-byes, a tearful but deeply painful letting go. Their grief is surely just as tangible as our loss of Shari, which was sudden . . . and, obviously, unexpected.

It was also cruel. The driver of the car was a teenager with no business behind the wheel of a car, for many reasons. She had no driver's license. She had no insurance. She was drunk out of her mind. And, as a mother, perhaps this was even harder for me to accept: This teen's own mom was also in the car. She was sprawled across the backseat so full of alcohol herself that she had handed over the keys to her inexperienced and also inebriated daughter.

I could have been filled with bitterness during the days, weeks and even years after this tragedy that left our three darling granddaughters motherless and our devoted son-in-law without his loving wife. But our family chose to make bitterness our enemy rather than the drunks whose car crashed into Shari. We'd seen what bitterness can do and knew it to be a tool of Satan, an effective way to make a very bad situation much, much worse. Bitterness can be far more destructive than rapidly reproducing cancer cells. It can demolish more lives than a hurricane, leaving a cruel and overwhelming sense of hopelessness in its wake. It's the nuclear bomb of feelings, killing everyone, because bitterness demolishes the spirit—our core as human beings made in the image of God.

We chose forgiveness. I will tell you why . . . and how.

Thanksgiving 2001

Our country was only a few weeks beyond the terrorist attacks of 9/11 when our family gathered as usual for that great American tradition called Thanksgiving. Like other Americans that day—indeed, people everywhere who love freedom and peace—we sensed the pall cast over the nation's usual celebration. America was hurting.

By November the embers were barely cooling at Ground Zero, site of the once towering World Trade Center buildings. Workers were repairing a large section of the Pentagon near Washington, DC. Yet people felt anxious. Would Al-Qaida attack again? Would they pick other obvious targets, or would they hit us in the heartland, perhaps selecting a school or a shopping mall or some other public location where innocent citizens were returning to everyday lives of normalcy . . . and hope?

On that Thanksgiving, we as a family felt a special intentionality about our thankfulness. We were together. We were safe. We could laugh and feel joy. The spontaneity of children and young adults allowed me to suspend my focus on the national tragedy of recent weeks. On that day, life was full of promise, not destruction. Life surrounded us. Death did not exist.

Our Thanksgiving feast was at noon that Thursday. Like many families, our children had invitations from other relatives and in-laws, so they would soon scoot out the door. But Shari, as usual, lingered. Her habit for at least a decade had been to decorate my Christmas tree after the Thanksgiving meal. Because we lived on Galveston Bay, we used a nautical theme. With her artistic eye, Shari began placing the fishnet swags, buoys and sailboats. She carefully wrapped each branch of the tree with lights. It was nearly 4 P.M. when her husband, Jeff, reminded her that they needed to leave for his parents' home. Shari said, "Just a minute. I'm almost finished." Then she placed the last ornament in exactly the right spot and stepped back to make sure the effect was perfect.

It had been a good day. My fall First Place 4 Health session was nearly over, and Shari, who was in my class, had brought a sugar-free pumpkin pie so that she and I could share a healthy dessert. Now, with the Christmas tree decorated, it was time for Shari, Jeff and their three girls to head over to the home of her in-laws. We hugged good-bye.

A Frantic Telephone Call

Here are the facts we learned of what happened that evening in a frantic phone call from granddaughter Cara, who was 19.

After dinner, Shari and her husband and daughters settled into their car to drive home. Suddenly, Shari remembered some items she wanted to give to Jeff's mom, so she stepped from their Expedition and went to the back to retrieve the items. Jeff's mom was standing behind the vehicle with Shari when a fast-moving car suddenly jumped the curb and headed down the sidewalk toward them. Just before impact, the car swerved, hit a light pole and ricocheted hard into Shari, throwing her onto the front lawn.

Shari's leg had been severed from her body, and she was bleeding badly. Jeff held her in his arms while an ambulance and other first responders screeched to the scene. Shari sat up just a bit and said to Jeff, "Tell the girls I love them."

In the midst of the chaos, Cara had the presence of mind to check on the condition of the people in the car that had hit Shari. They were too inebriated to make much sense, but we later learned they were not injured. Cara even felt inclined to share Christ with the driver, who by then was sitting in a drunken stupor in the back of a police car. This insight into the behavior of Cara—and her sisters, Christen, 15, and Amanda, 13—gives you some idea of their strong upbringing in the Christ-centered home of Shari and Jeff.

I was tired and had gone to bed early. At 9:15 P.M., I answered Cara's frantic call while Johnny relaxed on the patio, visiting with two of his brothers. We rushed to the hospital, calling our other two children as we drove. When we arrived, Shari was in surgery. We were gathered in the family room when the chaplain came in to tell us that Shari had not survived.

God's Love Is Enough

Besides our relatives, we have a large extended family. One honorary member is Beth Moore, the author and teacher of numerous Bible studies. Beth and I have poured our lives into the same church for three decades. Shari's youngest daughter, Amanda, was the first to realize the importance of having Beth among us during our agonizing stay at the hospital. At Amanda's urging, someone thought to contact Beth, who jumped in her car and headed right over.

In the foreword to my book titled *The Mother-Daughter Legacy* (co-authored by me and granddaughter Cara), Beth Moore wrote, "I made it to the hospital right after Jesus had swept Shari into His arms. As I stole just a moment alone with her and brushed the hair out of her stilled face, I thought of how He had just been standing in that very room. I inhaled to see if His fragrance still lingered."[1]

We invited Beth to speak at Shari's service. Jeff supplied Beth with copies of her own Bible studies that Shari had completed. On the pages were Shari's answers to questions, plus her other handwritten comments. Jeff figured that reading them might help Beth prepare for the funeral. It turned out to be a wonderful idea. For example, Beth read from several of Shari's notations, giving all of us who filled that sanctuary a sense of Shari's deep heart for God. Here is a prayer Shari wrote: "Thank you, Lord, for wanting to spend time with me each day. That was your plan. You are enough."[2]

God's love *is* enough. It will see us through unspeakable tragedies, heartaches and events that threaten to unravel our very existence. In a few paragraphs you will read the first-person account of a man who went through an experience (of a much different nature) that was as devastating to him as Shari's death was to us.

The link between his story and ours can be captured in one word: forgiveness.

A Story of Forgiveness

We chose to forgive those two inebriated women in the car that took Shari's life. Or to state it more directly: Their bad choices are what caused her death.

On the one-year anniversary of Shari's death, the *Houston Chronicle* sent a reporter to write a follow-up story. From her questions we could tell that her angle was "bitterness." Were we bitter that the teenage driver was given only a 12-year prison sentence? Did we hold a grudge against the irresponsible mother who passed off the car keys to her also drunk daughter, who wasn't even licensed to drive? "Of course, they escaped the accident without a scratch," noted the reporter. "How do you feel about that?"

I think we surprised the reporter when we told her that—in the previous 12 months—we had prayed for the driver and her mother, asking God to reach out to them, to touch them and to help them make something of their lives.

Our Lord, after all, has forgiven us . . . over and over again.

The verse at the beginning of this chapter, Matthew 6:14, is convicting: "For if you forgive men when they sin against you, your heavenly Father will also forgive you." I also want you to know the wording of verse 15 that follows it: "But if you do not forgive men their sins, your Father will not forgive your sins."

As my precious daughter Lisa puts it, "People can choose to live a life of bitterness. It will always rob them of joy. And the joy is available to them, if they realize what God has done by forgiving us. And He gives us the power to extend that forgiveness to others."

Forgiveness restores hope.

Another Real-life Story

A man who prefers to go by the name "Jeremy" in this book agreed to share the following. His candor may bring you to tears, yet I think you'll be blessed by his story of the awesome power of forgiveness. Later in *Hope 4 You*, I will share the incredible experience of his wife, Jennifer.

"Jeremy's" Story

God has blessed me with incredible grace. But before telling you the details of that story, I will explain some background.

I was raised in the church. All the members of my immediate family are committed believers, including almost everyone on my mother's side of the family (more than 80).

Today I would describe my current phase of spiritual development as growing and maturing. When people ask me to describe what it means to be a Christian, here's what I say: It is simple and complex all at the same time.

It simply means "accepting" (considering, understanding, appreciating) the free gift of Jesus Christ and the "work" He did on the cross for me, which was to sacrifice His life in place of mine so that all my sins (past, present and future) are forgiven. In other words, I don't deserve forgiveness, because I can't possibly earn it, which is the concept of "grace"—receiving something without earning it. This is because God is loving, yet He is also just. Nothing we can do will literally make up for the sins we commit as humans, so *He lovingly grants to us our salvation*, which serves to balance His scales of perfect justice. This gift allows me to share eternal life with Jesus my Savior and God the Father and to be guided by the Holy Spirit during my time on earth. I made this decision as a child and rededicated my life to Christ as an adult when I began to understand it better.

The complex part of being a Christian is how, throughout our lives, we constantly battle the flesh and sin through the concept of God's free will, which is His generous offer for us to act on our own decisions. As we mature in our faith, we find that those decisions always involve "letting go"—letting Jesus lead us. This has been very tough for me.

You may ask: Have I submitted to the Lordship of Jesus Christ? Yes, I have. I find this is both a decision and a process. I made the decision early as a child and recommitted to it when I was in college. But the process is lifelong and daily. It's a continual struggle to get out of the driver's seat and allow Him to lead, steer and guide me to where He wants me to go. Sometimes I am successful at doing this, and other times I am not.

I'll backtrack a bit. According to my mother, I was born with a temper, red hair and all. My mom never worked while we were young, and so we were fortunate to have her around all the time. On the other hand, my dad worked most of the time. I am not sure what his absence meant to me during those years. He was a good father. We did things together, but I don't remember him being around much. My dad was a good provider, and I think he felt that the long work hours were his way of loving us.

I was a good student and became bored with school and teachers pretty easily. It was during my first years of grade school that my dad led me to make a profession of faith that Jesus is my Savior, and I was baptized in a backyard pool.

In junior high, I was starting to notice girls and become conscious of what others thought of me. During my entire time growing up, my parents had us in church on Sundays and in Awana or youth group on Wednesday nights. I could see my mom working on her relationship with God, but the visible spiritual leadership from my dad was something I did not observe as much, mostly due to his long work hours. Although a very moral man, he did not personally emphasize much spiritual training in our home that I can remember.

During this time, I excelled at school and at sports. I made friends easily, but I worked harder at that than on my relationship with the Lord. I was a Sunday-morning Christian. I was not developing a Christian worldview to the extent that I talked about it or could defend it, but the Lord continued to pour good values into my life through godly Christian men. I did not develop consistent Bible study habits (and have had difficulty developing them now that I am older). My dad was busy, and my mom was struggling to keep the family going spiritually. I really tasted more freedom than I should have. I doubt if I was known to any of my friends as a Christian.

After my sophomore year, our family moved to another state. I remember thinking about my life at this point and thanking God for the opportunity to start over. I would make new friends. I would really try to live a "Christian life." At some level, I knew that I wasn't living the life that God wanted me to live. Unfortunately, any commitment to change didn't last long, because I was trying to make the changes myself instead of letting the Lord do them.

Yet, I was in church on Sundays, learning about Jesus Christ. The Lord was with me, and His hand was on my life. I look back now at the desires of my heart and praise God that He didn't allow me to experience as many of them as He could have. I was protected. I did experience things that I wish I hadn't, but God used those things to mold me and shape me into the person I am today. And the key is that He forgave me for those things long before I even thought of doing them.

I couldn't wait for college. I pursued that with everything I had. After a disappointing letter from the Air Force Academy, I moved 400 miles away from home and worked for a year preparing for school. During that year of being on my own, the Lord began to really change me. I rededicated my life to Him. I surrounded myself with Christian friends. I began to walk in a closer relationship with the Lord.

At the same time, Satan attacked me even harder. College led to some immoral choices, but God was good to me. Again, the Lord got hold of my heart, and I began the process of letting go of my life and giving it to Him. It has come one piece at a time, and I am convinced that there are still areas in my life today that I continue to hold on to. The Lord is identifying where they are, and I have to pry open my hands and give those areas to Him. Philippians 1:6 is the key verse in my struggle to give God what is really His: "Being confident of this, that he who began a good work in you will carry it on to completion until the day of Christ Jesus." I can't think of a better verse for me. And, amazingly enough, neither could my mom. This is the verse that the Lord gave to her as she prayed for me during my growing-up years.

In my second year of college, I met this beautiful girl who loved the Lord and who actually thought I wasn't so bad. Eighteen months later we were married, and I left school and my football scholarship, with two years left to finish my degree.

Coming into marriage, both people bring their own experiences, expectations and baggage. We were no different. I had a mother who liked to do things for me, and so figuring out how to pull my own weight at home was a learning process. I also came to marriage with a wandering eye, struggling with wanting things that weren't mine, and I was deathly afraid of losing this battle and allowing myself to get sucked into an affair.

My wife grew up in a dysfunctional family. Her father left her mother when she was two or three, and they bounced around, living with different men until the Lord got hold of her mother and soon-to-be stepfather. He was an alcoholic, and she was abusive. During her high school years, my wife found friendship with a local church family and eventually moved in with them. She exchanged the mental and verbal abuse from her own family for what became spiritual abuse with the new family. Eventually, she had to be taken forcibly from that situation and deprogrammed by a cult specialist. By God's grace, she was freed from the chains of this spiritual abuse only days before she was scheduled to fly away with a missionary whom the family friends had introduced to her. The FBI later confirmed that this "missionary" was not who he said he was and that the ticket was actually one-way to Germany and a suspected "white slavery" ring.

After some intensive counseling, we were married. I decided to leave school for a while, so we moved away from home and from our support network. We were on an adventure, living in the Rocky Mountains and skiing every day. However, our first year was very dry spiritually, and I was learning "on the job" how to be a good husband. My wife was learning to cope with her new role, and neither of us understood the art of communication. She fell prey to the advances of a co-worker with a willing ear and had a brief affair in the weeks leading up to our first anniversary.

We separated but were still very much in love with each other. The honeymoon was barely over, and as painful as that period was, it was also easier to forgive and forget. We got a little counseling (too little) and moved on.

A few months later, our first child was conceived and life settled into a new rhythm surrounded by all the excitement and new experiences of becoming parents. We quickly realized that our lives were to be very different and the "fun" jobs, making little money, needed to change. We moved back to the Midwest where I returned to college to finish my degree. I worked full-time (nights) and went to school during the day. Somehow we made it through that schedule, and I graduated with honors. We buried the baggage as much as possible and moved on. Unfortunately, this kind of baggage seems to find its way back to the surface, making it easy to trip over again.

Fast-forward 10 years. Our family had expanded to four kids, and we were contentedly living in the western U.S. and working in a Christian-related business. My career was in a great place, and we loved the area. The money was pretty good as the economy was flying. Having an entrepreneurial bent, I opened a real estate investment business and we also decided to buy a fast-food franchise to run as a family enterprise.

My wife recently had been diagnosed with depression and was under the care of a Christian counselor (and friend). She was unpacking the baggage she had not really dealt with from growing up and from the stress of being a full-time mom and wife. As we both learned, depression is a chemical imbalance and sometimes needs to be treated with medication. My wife grudgingly began to accept this as part of the healing process.

These were busy times for our family, and, of course, 20/20 hindsight makes things so much clearer. I was working a full-time job, leading a sales division for a product manufacturing company. My job took me away on frequent business trips. When I was home, our other interests in real estate and the franchise kept me pretty occupied. I was blinded by all the effort and stuff in my life and didn't see the storm clouds gathering on the horizon.

At one point, I left the country for a business trip in Europe. I was flying back with a colleague when I got an urgent voice message from my boss after we had just been ushered through customs in Chicago.

"Call me. Your wife is in the hospital, and we have the kids." I quickly called him back and was able to grab a couple of additional details. She had tried to take her life. The county had intervened and had her locked down in the psychiatric wing. I couldn't talk to her or see her. And my boss told me, "She doesn't want to talk to you. Get home as soon as possible."

I was stunned. I knew something was really wrong, and after I boarded the last flight home, I broke down crying on the plane. In my heart, I knew what had happened.

As part of the process of buying the franchise, we had to attend two weeks of training at the company headquarters in order to learn about the company, how to prepare the food, work with the marketing programs, and so forth. We'd hired a general manager, and my wife was attending as head of operations. She traveled to the national headquarters for the training. I could sense a distance developing in our relationship but had no idea why or what to do, so, in typical fashion, I buried myself in other work.

The toll of our stress, her depression and my inattentiveness helped release some of her inhibition, and she began an affair with the corporate trainer that lasted for several weeks. The guilt became unbearable and led to her attempt on her life. She got to the point where she walked away from everything that had been important to her.

Pain, anger, confusion . . . all are part of the process that someone goes through when infidelity invades a marriage relationship. I had them in spades. My mom flew out on an emergency flight from the Midwest, and I ran away for almost a week. It was during this time of soul searching that I came to grips with what had happened and realized I was part of the problem.

After returning home, I began counseling with my pastor, and we discussed the options. We talked about how I'd contributed to the situation we were in. We talked about what the Bible says about infidelity and divorce. All I knew at the time was that my wife had taken my heart and crushed it, and she didn't want to see me. It hurt so much, because I still loved her. This separation went on for almost a month before the counselors arranged our first meeting together. Little did I know what I was about to be faced with as the meeting unfolded.

We walked into the counselor's office, and the first thing that struck me was how many people had gathered in that little room. Some very close friends were there, along with our pastor and the counselor. It was the first time I had seen my wife in a month, and she looked very miserable. I was trying to keep an open mind to whatever was going to happen. I didn't know how to react. A part of me wanted to get very angry. A part of me wanted to throw it all away. Yet, I knew that wasn't what God wanted ultimately, even though I was pretty sure that He and I weren't on the same page.

After some ground rules were laid down, I read my wife a letter I had written, pouring out my pain and anger at what she'd done, not only to me but to our kids. And then my wife read me a letter she'd written. She said she was sorry for all the pain she'd caused and that she had something else to share. She was pregnant.

I was rocked. The baby couldn't be mine. I'd had a vasectomy four years earlier. What was she saying? Then it hit me. She was pregnant with the other man's child.

I sat there for what seemed like five minutes (probably only a few seconds), then I simply got up and walked out the door. I thought, *This is it. I'm done. How can I be expected to live with that? She's on her own.* I wanted to curse God. In fact, I remember looking up at the night sky and screaming at Him, "Why?"

And then, very gently, I heard a voice. I have never heard the Lord audibly before or since, but I swear that I heard Him gently ask me a simple question: "Did I forgive you?"

I began to argue with Him in my thoughts, but the more they swirled, the quicker I realized what my Savior was asking me: When I laid my life before Him and believed in His saving power and His blood that He shed on the cross for my sins, did I *really* believe all of that in my heart? If so, then He was asking: If I fully understood the significance of what He had done on my behalf, could I, in turn, forgive my wife?

At that moment, it was as if a switch was turned in my heart. I don't know how else to describe it. I suddenly and fully realized that Jesus Christ had ransomed His life for mine by dying on the cross for my sins, all of them, and He, in turn, wanted me and my wife to experience His incredible unconditional love *through the tangible act of my forgiving her*. Furthermore, He would be there to perform this miraculous work through me. And now the rest of the story . . .

My wife and I began the healing process through much counseling and prayer, and she had a similar experience to mine in that she came to a true and healing knowledge of God's grace in her life. For the first time, she began not only to claim God's promises but to embrace them as her own personal grace and forgiveness. A couple of months later, we were "re-married" on our original anniversary and spent that day with family and friends, including having our four kids stand up with us as we took our new vows.

We both felt very strongly that, as part of our healing process, we needed to give the baby to an adoptive family. We knew of a Christian couple who had struggled with their own journey of childlessness, and we were able to bless them with the joy of doctor's visits, prenatal care and, ultimately, a delivery. They took a baby girl home and gave her a beautiful, biblical name that reflects God's grace. We still keep in touch with that family and get to look "in the window" from time to time as they post photos online. From the moment we made that decision, my wife sensed that she was carrying the baby for this couple. So, by the grace of God, she never had to deal with the emotional consequences that sometimes occur because of giving up a baby for adoption.

Our other four children experienced the pregnancy and birth right along with us and will someday know the truth behind the circumstances that led us both on that journey. For now, they know that Mom and Dad were blessed with a baby so that we could bless another family. They know that they are loved and cherished and wanted.

My wife and I have been married almost 18 years in total, and we'll celebrate our special sixth anniversary this year as well. We have four wonderful kids, and the Lord has taught us many important lessons. I have to die to myself every day, and there are days when I fail. However, the Lord is gracious, and He loves me anyway. My desire is to live a life pleasing to Him and to pass along this rich spiritual heritage to my children. I want them to know Him because of what He has done for me. I want them to see me spending time with Him. I want to introduce them to His Word.

That is my mission field.

For Study

1. Fill in the blanks in this chapter's Scripture verse, plus the verse that follows it.

   For if you forgive men when they _______ against you, your heavenly Father will also ______________ you. But if you do ____ forgive men their sins, your Father will not forgive _______ sins (Matt. 6:14-15).

2. In this chapter we discussed how forgiveness can replace bitterness, restoring hope. Obviously, this is a choice, an action and a process. Describe how this has worked in your life.

   ____

   ____

   ____

   ____

   ____

3. Jeremy's testimony included a description of the salvation process, which includes God forgiving you through the act of His Son, Jesus, dying in your place as atonement for your sins. If you feel certain that you understand this and have taken the step of trusting God (instead of your own efforts) for your salvation, describe how you *know* that God has forgiven you.

____

____

____

____

____

____

If you have not taken this step, and you would like to do so now, please write a prayer in the space provided. Some sample wording is contained in the prayer below.

____

____

____

____

____

____

Dear God, thank You for sending Your Son, Jesus, to show me the way to live from now on. Thank You for loving me unconditionally and for the truly awesome gift of accepting my sins as forgiven, because Jesus died in my place. Whether this is the first time or the hundredth time I have paused to think of this and thank You for it, I am still overwhelmed by the power of that sacrifice and the grace You have extended to me for a full and satisfying life of service to You here on earth, and an eternal life with You after I die. Amen.

7

Thankfulness Rekindles Hope

Give thanks in all circumstances, for this is God's will for you in Christ Jesus.
1 THESSALONIANS 5:18

Depending on what's going on in your life as you read this, today's Scripture could make total sense to you or it may seem like nonsense. Let's explore some scenarios.

Perhaps today feels like a brand-new day but also a new season of life because you received some wonderful news. Maybe a life crisis finally has been resolved, or it's something as mundane as completing a task you keep putting off. It could be nothing more complex than a morning of sunshine after days of rain. While the rain might have been needed, the cloudy days could have dampened your mood—and today's dry warmth pulls you outdoors like flowers drawn to the sun.

It's easy to feel thankful at times like this . . . and, especially, to see God's hand in our mood of rekindled hope. We feel gratitude and, hopefully, will express it to the Lord with a prayer of thanksgiving. Or we may acknowledge His generosity to others by attributing our positive feelings or our sense of accomplishment to God's provision and guidance in our life. (In addition, and many would say this is more important, we will acknowledge our gratitude to God through our witness to others about Him and through our Christlike actions.)

However, life is messy, isn't it? And no matter how good our intentions—or even how deep our faith—sometimes life overwhelms us and we have a hard time feeling thankful. See if you can relate to any of these . . .

Perhaps your child or grandchild is in serious trouble because of bad influences; one result is that you're overcome with fear. Or you're overwhelmed with a project at work, and you sense your job is at stake—now *that's* pressure. Maybe you've been given a scary diagnosis by your doctor, and suddenly you're faced with the first sense of your own mortality. Although older friends and relatives have died through the years, before your recent medical crisis, death to you was mostly theoretical.

How do *you* respond?

The Christian Response

Let's look at the context for Paul's direction to the church at Thessalonica, a bustling city of 200,000 in biblical times that served as an important seaport in an area known as Macedonia. That's today's modern Greece, and Thessalonica's culture, folklore and love of sports are still influencing the world (think Nike).

The notes in my *New International Version* Study Bible tell me that Paul wrote this letter around AD 51. It was among his earliest correspondence to infant churches. He wrote it for encouragement to the small group of converts—some Jews but mostly Gentiles—who needed support in the face of persecution from their fellow residents of this influential but pagan city.

As always when I select a verse for my chapters, I check the surrounding verses (plus other contextual information). I like the way Paul's words here are simple, direct and, oh, so relevant to people then and now who are seeking hope. Here's what he says in 1 Thessalonians 5:16-22: "Be joyful always; pray continually; give thanks in all circumstances, for this is God's will for you in Christ Jesus. Do not put out the Spirit's fire; do not treat prophecies with contempt. Test everything. Hold on to the good. Avoid every kind of evil."

Now try to imagine this group of new believers receiving Paul's letter. It's probable that some (or most) were not literate, and so they were dependent on others in their group to read and reread

Paul's words to them. Or maybe they couldn't read but had good minds, so they committed parts of his letter to memory.

In First Place 4 Health, we believe in strengthening our health in four ways: physically (our body), emotionally (our feelings), mentally (our mind or thinking abilities), spiritually (meaning our soul—sometimes referred to as our spirit—which encompasses our attitudes, responses, behaviors, and so forth). In First Place 4 Health, we strengthen our "mind" (literally, our brain) by memorizing Scripture, which is a workout that's just as relevant to our strength and overall health as an hour in the gym or a 30-minute walk through our neighborhood or during lunch hour at work.

"Dying Grace"

Now that we've brought these key verses into contemporary life, let's consider how many more tools we have to remind us of their truths and their application to our circumstances. I remember a detailed voicemail message I once heard. The caller informed me with heartbreak in his voice that a relatively young friend had died of a heart attack after an evening jog. I responded back with encouragement, also leaving voicemails. After the funeral, this man texted me that he and his wife were on their way home and that the experience had been "very good, even though it was very bad."

I knew what he meant, because I've experienced it myself with the passing of both my mother and my father, and certainly the death of our dear daughter Shari. I call it "dying grace." Somehow God's grace carries you through that terrible time. As a believer in Christ, you even find the ability to be thankful.

Maybe you are aware of seemingly insignificant details people shared with you at the funeral that carry great importance in your grief. You thank God for that person's words. When my aging mom came to live with us in 1999, one of the hardest three-year periods of my life began. She always had been my hero because of her can-do attitude and upbeat spirit. She deserved those, too, because she could fix anything that was broken and sew anything that needed mending. When she died on January 3, 2003, my friend Kay Smith said to me, "Carole, you have lost your greatest cheerleader." It was a bittersweet comment, but it made me thankful for the many years I enjoyed with my mother. My view of God as the perfect parent was shaped and molded early on from my experiences with my earthly mother, "the fixer," and my father, who was my "protector."

Thankful in All Circumstances

When we're in the midst of difficult circumstances—shock at the sudden death of a loved one, for example—we often don't realize how a close walk with the Lord prepares us to be thankful. This, to me, is the beauty of memorizing Scripture. Not only have we hidden the truth of God's Word in our heart, but the Holy Spirit also calls it to our attention by bringing a key verse to the surface of our grieving and overwhelmed mind. It's like our mental circuitry is exploding (I've also heard it described as "shutting down"), and yet we can live a truth of Scripture at that very moment.

When Beth Moore spoke at our daughter Shari's funeral, she told an amusing story about meeting a teacher of my granddaughter Amanda, Shari's youngest. Amanda had been late for school a number of times, and since Amanda was such a good student, the teacher asked her why she was sometimes tardy. The girl replied, "It's my mom. She can't get out of her Bible to get us here on time."

That caused a chuckle, of course, but what really brought me to an attitude of thankfulness was when a friend of mine said this after the service: "I need to make some big changes. I don't want to die and have my kids remember me sitting around reading romance novels."

Actually, I have a whole list of circumstances—both large and small—that happened around the time of Shari's tragic death that demonstrate the truth of being thankful in *all* circumstances. They also highlight a reason for hiding these truths in our heart so the Holy Spirit can access them when our circumstances change quickly. One of them may seem insignificant to you, but it wasn't to me.

It was the night of the viewing for Shari. I had not given a moment of thought to what I would wear. And, to be honest, I could not care less how I looked. But with that weight of resignation we feel at overwhelming times like this, I went to my closet. Immediately, my eyes fell on a silk pantsuit Shari and her sister had bought me for Christmas almost a year earlier. It was too tight at the time I opened the gift, but it was a very pretty green suit, and so I kept it rather than return it. I'd never worn it.

Feeling a tiny bit hopeful, I pulled it out of the closet and slipped it on. It fit perfectly! I thanked God and sensed a rekindling of my hope.

At the time of Shari's death, I never dreamed that thankfulness would be one of the resources God would use to heal the huge void left in my heart. I know that people grieve in different ways and that everyone is different; but I have come to believe that being thankful *in the midst of* tragic circumstances is the key to moving toward healing.[1]

Circumstances Change Quickly

I've told you some details about the devastation caused by Hurricane Ike in 2008. To provide an idea of how quickly circumstances can change, I'm going to excerpt from my journal during that time period.[2]

Week 1

August 25-31, 2008

We were anticipating the landfall of Hurricane Gustav somewhere between New Orleans and Galveston. New Orleans and our nation were spared catastrophic damage [because Gustav weakened to levels categorized as tropical storm and tropical depression].

Our kids came to the Bay over the weekend to help us load Johnny's cargo trailer. We are going to store it away from our home on high ground until hurricane season is over around the end of

November. [Family members] were going to load all of my mom's boxes into the trailer when someone said: "Let's not do this again. Let's go through the boxes and dispose of this stuff once and for all." We worked from 8 A.M. until midnight, only stopping for meals. Praise God, we finished the task that I have thought about and worried about since 1999!

I wrote the Introduction and first two chapters of Give God a Year. *I talked with Bill Greig, president of Gospel Light, about the book being published by the end of 2009.*

We looked at seven possible office spaces, getting ready for the change from being a ministry of Houston's First Baptist Church to a non-profit 501(c)(3) corporation.

I received so many answers to prayer this week—Cara and Luke, no hurricane, and Mom's things disposed of after almost 10 years of moving the boxes around. Great meetings, got so much work done, Johnny felt good all week.

Completed all seven items on my list every day! Yeah!

Lost 5 pounds!!!

Week 2

September 1-7, 2008

Wrote two more chapters for Give God a Year.

Completed all seven items on my list every day!

Saturday I hand washed my car and bathed the dog. Bought groceries, colored my hair, watered the flowers. Ate healthy all day.

Got up before 3:00 A.M. three days this week to write and haven't experienced fatigue one minute. This is a miracle, as I normally need seven to eight hours of sleep a night. God is doing something here and multiplying my sleep in the process.

Got up at 2:30 A.M. Sunday to write and prepare to worship in our brand-new sanctuary today. I am meeting two persons who haven't attended church in a while.

Proposal for First Place 4 Health to become 501(c)(3) was unanimously approved by Deacon Administrative Committee.

Week 3

September 8-14, 2008

The week started out well, and I finished chapter 6 of Give God a Year.

On Wednesday we received word that Hurricane Ike was heading for Galveston, so we began the process of packing up to leave. John and Lisa came on Wednesday to help us pack; they moved all our plants and lawn furniture into the garage and took the boat back to Houston when they left. Our friends Nick and Euphanel Goad called on Thursday morning and left word for us to evacuate to their retreat center at Round Top. I called Euphanel to see if our pets could come and she said, "Bring them, too." We were able to get Archie, one of our two cats, into a carrier, but the other one, Yellow Cat, shot out the door, so he stayed at the Bay because we were unable to coax him back into the house.

On Friday night, Hurricane Ike came into Galveston, and its path came right over our home. Early Saturday morning our next-door neighbors, Greg and Melissa Jones, drove down to the Bay. They had to walk more than two miles because the roads were flooded, but they were able to take pictures of the area as they walked. They both knew what they were going to find before they ever got to our house, because every home they saw that was ground level was gutted by the storm surge. Melissa and Greg's home was fine, because it was new and built on pilings. The downstairs was destroyed, but they didn't even have a picture crooked on the wall upstairs.

Melissa called me from San Leon, and she was sobbing so hard I could barely understand her. She told me that our home was destroyed. That night Greg and Melissa drove to Round Top to personally show us the photos. Greg said, "There was no way I was going to email these to you." They spent the night with us, along with our family who had traveled to Round Top so we could all be together.

Thank You, Lord!

As for the above peek into my life at the time of Hurricane Ike, many of you readers have been through such circumstances and far worse.

My point in sharing notations from my journal is to demonstrate how rapidly our circumstances change and how quickly the causes of shock and grief pile up.

One week I was dealing with boxes of belongings left over from my mom's death—an emotional endeavor but one that carried the reward of "getting something important finished." The next week I was cheerfully covering the gray in my hair, watering my flowers, washing my dog and my car—life seemed just grand. The next week a hurricane destroyed our home and washed most of our belongings into Galveston Bay.

But here's the truth: Life *was* grand at times during all of those circumstances. A closer look at my journal notations reveals reasons among the chaos to be profoundly thankful:

- I'm so grateful the kids took with them all the family photos before the storm.
- I had been collecting pottery of a type we received as wedding gifts in 1959, buying up pieces on eBay. An entire upper cabinet in the kitchen was still intact and full of the pottery.
- We found Yellow Cat on the rafters in (what was left of) the garage but were unable to coax him down. On Wednesday we went back to the Bay with a can of tuna and the cat carrier. We were able to retrieve Yellow Cat and take him back to Round Top. At least now we have all of our family together!
- Our daughter Lisa and her husband, Kent, came up to Round Top because they had no electricity and so now we have a cook. Thank You, Lord!

And from my journal about three months after Ike:

> *Being homeless makes you think about what you want to move, so I can see why homeless people carry all their worldly possessions in a shopping cart or on their backs. I get a mental picture of us, if we were homeless, walking Meathead on a leash, with two cat car-*

riers and a birdcage in a big wagon dragging along behind us. My sense of humor is a little jaded right now; I think the magnitude of our loss is settling in after three months of dealing with it.

As I work on this chapter for *Hope 4 You*, today's emails include one from a dear friend who recounts how she and her husband have lost someone close to them every spring season for the past five years. Some of these deaths have been within days of a very happy event, such as a son's wedding and a grandchild's birth.

The life of a Christian can be a roller coaster. I shake my head when I think about people who, frankly, don't walk with the Lord and who sometimes think the life of a Christian must be very boring. It's more like living in an action movie!

More Real-life Stories

Vicki Heath handles leadership and fitness development for First Place 4 Health, speaking at conferences and doing whatever it takes to build strong leaders, especially the ones who can lead our fitness programs. This anecdote is another example of the connections among members of God's family. I'll let Vicki tell it in her own words.

Catherine Cutrell Peak

By Vicki Heath

We have a wonderful Body & Soul leader, Cathy Cutrell, whose daughter was diagnosed with stage IV breast cancer and not given much hope at all. (The daughter's name is Catherine Cutrell Peak, if you would care to pray for her.) Her story is such an encouragement for people who have been given a supposed death sentence by well-meaning doctors, yet over time the prayer partners learn that God has different plans.

When I heard about Catherine's diagnosis, I was utterly distraught. She has been a friend for many years. In fact, my pastor husband performed the marriage ceremony for Catherine and her husband, and as my good friend Cathy's daughter, Catherine has been almost like a daughter to me. She was diagnosed only four months after giving birth—so heartbreaking! Yet think how many people have been blessed with the opportunity to pray and to learn of God's individualized plan and care for her. (A divine mystery is why He chooses to leave some of us on earth for so much longer than others.)

Her latest prognosis has made my hope meter soar. Doctors say that at this time she is cancer free. I thank God for that! And I thank Him for Catherine's strong faith and her witness to His healing power.

The next two real-life examples will give you more insight into the deep heart for God tucked into my wonderful assistant, Pat. I wish every First Place 4 Health reader could meet her in person. Pat and I have different personalities, which may be one reason we get along so well. She is an integral part of the First Place 4 Health ministry. (She happens to have the same last name as mine, Lewis, but we're not related, although we're certainly sisters in Christ.)

The following is a piece she wrote more than a decade ago based on her reading of a book by Evelyn Christenson entitled *Lord, Change Me!*[3] Like all of us at one time or another, Pat was going through a troublesome period. She read Evelyn's very fine book and was inspired to write this essay.

The Blame Game

By Pat Lewis

"Lord, change *me?*

"Wait just a minute, Lord. You know it's my husband who needs changing, not me. He's the one who needs to be the spiritual leader of our family. I read my Bible, go to church, pray, and my life would be just fine if you would only change him."

After 25 years of marriage and three children near grown, I found myself discontented. During that time, someone gave me a book called *Lord, Change Me!* I love to read, so I picked it up one day, thinking that maybe, just maybe, I would get some insight on how to change my husband.

I had tried to change my husband, and he had tried to change me. As each of us stubbornly resisted change, it had created ongoing conflict.

As I continued to read, I kept talking to the Lord. I told Him, "If there *is* something that I need to change, I am willing." But I didn't know what changes I needed to make in my life. I was shy and retiring, while my husband was outgoing and sociable. I was a dutiful wife, taking responsibility for my home, the children and everything I thought a wife was obligated to do and be. Isn't that what the Bible teaches . . . to be "submissive to your husband" and a "keeper of the home"? He was a good provider and loved me and his children, but we were totally different in our personalities, likes and dislikes.

Somewhere in the midst of reading the book and meditating on my situation, I prayed, "Lord, please change my husband," and very quietly and gently, the Holy Spirit whispered in my ear, "There are some things in you that need to be changed. Your heart is dirty with bitterness, unforgiveness, resentment and a stubborn will."

I was stunned, but I knew instantly that it was the truth. My husband and I married at a young age and brought into the marriage all the baggage from our childhood. I was very sensitive, and through the years my spirit had been wounded with unkind words and the actions of others. Because I did not like conflict, I had unknowingly stored up all of these emotions and hurts in my heart.

Oswald Chambers says, in his devotional book *My Utmost for His Highest*, ". . . the Holy Spirit is the only one able to show what is wrong without hurting and wounding."

I had no idea what was hidden in my heart. I blamed my discontentment on my husband.

After the Holy Spirit revealed the contents of my heart, I confessed them as sin against God and asked Him to remove all the filth from my heart and to change me. I asked Him to heal my wounds and renew my marriage. I changed my focus from my husband to God. As I did this, miraculously, my husband began to change before my very eyes. He knew nothing of what was happening in my life, because I am a very private person and at that time did not share what God had shown me.

The amazing thing was that as my husband changed and began to seek God for his own life, I learned how God used just the things about his personality (that I wanted to change) in ministry to others. God showed me that He makes each of us as individuals and has a perfect plan uniquely designed for that person. God then works through us in different ways to accomplish His plan and purpose on this earth.

In the years that followed, God used my husband in ministry to many people through his special gifts of loving people and his boldness in prayer and counseling. As I turned my focus from my husband to God, He began to use me through my own quiet and behind-the-scenes personality.

Psalm 139:23-24 says, "Search me, O God, and know my heart; test me and know my anxious thoughts. See if there is any offensive way in me and lead me in the way everlasting."

God has a wonderful plan and purpose for each of our lives, using the special gifts and talents He gives us through our different personalities. He is waiting for us to quit blaming others for our lack of happiness, peace and joy and turn our focus to Him, who "gives generously to all without finding fault" (Jas. 1:5).

As you read in Pat's piece, "The Blame Game," we can ask God to change our circumstances. But sometimes He says, "I want to change *you*." When He does, a miracle happens and the people around us begin to change as well. Over the years, God changed Pat's heart *and* her circumstances. I feel so privileged to be able to interview some of my friends and family members for this book.

Interview with Pat

Carole: Your son lives with you, and soon, your mother. I think you're beginning to run your own nursing home, Pat!

Pat: Yes, my mom is in her nineties, lives in Arkansas and still drives. I'm going to move her to Houston to live with me and my son, Terry, who is in his fifties and has end-stage renal disease. He is on dialysis twice a week due to severe complications from diabetes.

Carole: You took care of your husband, Bill, and lost him in 2000 . . .

Pat: Bill died of complications from diabetes. Terry has some of the same diabetic issues that his father had.

Carole: . . . and now your mom will join you. You really did not plan on all this, my friend.

Pat: No, I didn't. My brother died at 48, and my sister in her early 60s. They lived in Arkansas where Mom lives now, and I thought they would live a long life and be there for Mom. And I never expected my son to have the same terrible disease as his father.

Carole: And yet, Pat, you seem filled with hope.

Pat: My hope is in the Lord. If all I had to look forward to was this life, it could be pretty grim, but God promised to be my husband, my father, my everything. I'm not walking this walk by myself, even after losing my husband. That's how I look at life now.

Carole: What makes you thankful?

Pat: It's the knowledge that one day I will see all my family and loved ones who have gone before me to heaven, because all of them have known the Lord and believed in Him as their Savior. I'm so very thankful for that.

For Study

1. Describe your current circumstances, good and bad. Perhaps your health is good, but your financial circumstances are not so good, or even bad. Perhaps you are satisfied with your selection of a church, because you are being fed and challenged there, but you feel dissatisfaction in your job. List as many of your circumstances as you can and characterize them on a scale of 1 to 10, with the higher numbers being good.

2. Pick a few of the circumstances you listed, at both ends of the good and bad scale, and describe why you can be thankful for them. Tell how giving thanks for these circumstances rekindles your hope.

3. Look back at your overall "hope meter" in chapter 1. Place an arrow on the hope meter here, updating it, if applicable, according to what you have learned about hopefulness. Jot notes to yourself, as you did earlier in the book.

Show me, dear Lord, how to be thankful in all circumstances. Help me to find the joy in all things. Assure me that all of my circumstances strengthen me to better serve Your purposes for my life. Thank You. Amen.

8

Working with God

Do not put your hope in wealth, but put your hope in God.
1 TIMOTHY 6:17 (PARAPHRASE)

I don't know much about the rules of football, but I live in Texas where the attention on sports is huge and players are revered. So, as a Texan, I'd have to be living in a cave not to know that this week—while I'm writing this chapter—the NFL's annual draft of new players will be announced.

We've got our eyes on some players from Texas. One is Colt McCoy, the quarterback who took the University of Texas at Austin all the way to the national championship game. Not only is he a great athlete and a superb leader of teammates, but he also speaks publicly about his faith in Christ. In every after-game interview, he gives God the credit for his athletic abilities. Think of the millions of people who see a great football player humble himself in that way!

Just across the Red River is McCoy's archrival—yet another brother in the Lord—the quarterback from the University of Oklahoma, Sam Bradford. A Heisman Trophy winner in 2008, when he was only a sophomore Sooner, he currently holds the NCAA record for touchdown passes by a freshman, with 36. Bradford publicly gives God the credit for his athletic skills. Before the game he prepares for each match on the gridiron by reading the story in the Bible of David and Goliath.

A personal favorite of mine is Tim Tebow, quarterback for the Florida Gators and a Heisman Trophy winner. He's one of those players who literally wears his faith on his face—he applies a Scripture reference in his eye black on game day. It's thrilling to imagine the many people watching him as he drops back to pass and searches downfield for a receiver. Often a big play includes a close-up of the quarterback. In the case of Tebow, they see that Scripture reference so boldly visible on his cheeks. And here's the good part: I have a feeling a lot of those viewers jot down the reference, get out their Bibles and then look it up. (Okay, they probably wait for a commercial to do that, but that's good enough for me!) According to Google, they logged 94 million searches for John 3:16 when Tebow used that verse in his eye black for the 2009 BCS game against Oklahoma resulting in a National Championship title for the Gators.

Are you surprised that I would write about football quarterbacks in a chapter beginning with Scripture on putting your hope in God rather than wealth? I paraphrased the verse earlier. Here's how 1 Timothy 6:17 reads in the *New International Version*: "Command those who are rich in this present world not to be arrogant nor to put their hope in wealth, which is so uncertain, but to put their hope in God, who richly provides us with everything for our enjoyment." Here are verses 18 and 19: "Command them to do good, to be rich in good deeds, and to be generous and willing to share. In this way they will lay up treasure for themselves as a firm foundation for the coming age, so that they may take hold of the life that is truly life."

Professional football players are paid millions of dollars. How can they possibly be worth that much money?

Think of these three young quarterbacks who will move from the ranks of the college players to the highly paid pros. Soon they will earn annual paychecks with many zeroes, far more money than most of us will see in a lifetime. What will it do to them? Will it corrupt them? Or will they use it wisely for the kingdom of God, which they claim is their highest priority?

Hope in God

I pray that I'm right about what I'm going to say about these quarterbacks, three young men who are in the spotlight. They state publicly that they put their hope *first* in God. I firmly believe they will continue to place their hope in God above the great wealth that will surely become theirs. In fact, I believe they will use their financial gain for others—glorifying Him. They already do this by lending their names to ministries and by setting up foundations for biblically based causes, using endorsement money they could pocket for themselves.

Colt McCoy, for example, gives his Christian story in the "I Am Second" spots, which tell online viewers why he plays—and lives—for the Lord. It's exciting to see his familiar face on highway billboards with the "I Am Second" website listed, encouraging drivers who see the ad to log on. They hear him say in his own voice that his "highest priority is to serve God" by always trying to use *with excellence* the gifts He has provided.

Sam Bradford describes himself on the "I Am Second" website as a "perfectionist" who puts too much pressure on himself, adding that he always senses the presence of the Lord on the football field. He warns fans that, when people put themselves before God, "that's when their lives start unraveling." What mature advice from one who, as a consistent winner, easily could be less than humble.

Tim Tebow was a well-known figure even before he and his remarkable mother made a commercial that appeared during Super Bowl 2010. Focus on the Family, a highly successful Christian ministry that empowers families to serve God by growing and maintaining a faith-centered family life, sponsored the commercial. Imagine that! A ministry having the resources—and the vision—to place an ad on the most watched program on television!

The commercial allowed Tim and his mom to briefly tell their story of how she made a choice to give birth to him. If viewers followed up and went to the Focus on the Family website, they learned that Mrs. Tebow was seriously ill during her pregnancy and doctors advised her to terminate the pregnancy. She made a choice and chose life.

Imagine football without Tim Tebow. Imagine how his life has enriched the lives of other athletes and fans. Seeing that commercial was a proud moment for those who believe that God is the author of all life (even unborn); that He is the One who decides when life will begin and end.

As national director of First Place 4 Health, I must note that Colt McCoy, Sam Bradford and Tim Tebow are in tremendous physical shape, even though they have suffered career-threatening injuries. Colt McCoy wrenched the shoulder of his valuable throwing arm in his final college game, putting him in the locker room with doctors. Many Texas Longhorn fans I know say that is why his team did not win the national championship game against the victorious Alabama Crimson Tide. Sam Bradford also had a shoulder injury that kept him out for part of his last year at OU. Tim Tebow suffered a concussion and a fractured hand as a player at Florida and even finished a high school game on a broken leg.

Yet these three young men have managed to regain the physical health necessary to play football on pro teams. All three have great parental role models with solid, long-term marriages, plus divine leading from the Lord as encouragement to work on all four areas of health: emotional, mental and spiritual, as well as physical.

Later in the chapter you will read my interview with a friend who served as emcee at a dinner where Tebow was the speaker. I think you'll find her comments insightful.

Working with Excellence

You may not have millions of television and stadium fans cheering for you as you go about your work. But my prayer for you, dear reader, is that your day job is fulfilling. I also pray that you don't seek your *hope* in your day job. If so, I believe it will be misplaced hope.

When I say "day job," I'm including not just people who work outside their homes, but retirees who do volunteer work or contribute to their grandchildren's upbringing, plus all those busy homemakers, parents and caretakers who are home during the day, managing their household and taking care of their family but not earning a paycheck.

In our society we place too much emphasis on our value as paycheck earners. But that's not where our hope lies; our hope lies in the Lord. But as His servants, we also may be employees. If so, we should be doing our paying job with excellence, as a way to glorify Him.

I would be the most despondent, hopeless woman alive if I depended on my day job for my hope! I believe that, if I remain strong and healthy, I will be able to serve God for many more years, unless He takes me home (and that would be good too).

My goal as a "worker" is to make my personal life and my professional life seamless. In other words, I seek to serve the Lord whether I am employed in my professional capacity as national director of First Place 4 Health or working to help hurting women, a personal ministry role I also play.

I was greatly influenced by Henry Blackaby's landmark Bible study entitled *Experiencing God*. He and Claude King unpacked a series of principles that turned my world upside down. In that study, I learned that my life's work—whether paid or not—should be (1) finding out what God is doing in the world and (2) seeking to join Him in His work. This is the essence of working with God. I must figure out what gifts He has given me so that I can improve on them in every way possible and apply them to His ongoing work. And I must do that work with excellence, because I am a child of the King.

Jobs come and jobs go. Businesses fail. Bosses and leaders make mistakes. This is the reality of *any* day job. I have to be realistic, and so must you. If and when my day job ends, I will continue to work with God, the constant Source of my hope.

Real-life Stories

As promised, here is my interview with Becky Turner, who met Tim Tebow, one of the football players I wrote about with a compelling story regarding his relationship with the Lord. Becky is a neighbor and friend of mine who has achieved great success in the First Place 4 Health program. A capable and highly trained management professional, she speaks often to our First Place 4 Health groups and motivates participants to be successful.

Carole: I love your Facebook posts, Becky. A few days ago you wrote that "Tim Tebow is ROCK SOLID in his faith in Jesus! And pretty cute, too!" You even posted a photo of you standing next to him to prove your last remark. (You looked fabulous, too, by the way.) Tell us how you met this quarterback who is so outspoken about his faith.

Becky: Thanks, Carole. I had the privilege of serving as emcee at the annual gala for The Source for Women, a Houston-based organization that empowers abortion-vulnerable women to make informed choices when faced with an unwanted pregnancy. We were raising money to add the highest technology sonogram equipment available to our reproductive health counseling center. This is an effective tool for showing even newly pregnant women that the "Fetus" growing inside them is actually a living, breathing baby with fingers and toes—all the parts of human beings, because that's what they are. We're highly motivated to get that message out there, because Houston is now home to the second largest abortion clinic in the world, now that Planned Parenthood has finished building it. I understand that the largest abortion clinic is in China where the government mandates abortions.

Carole: So you raised lots of money and Tim Tebow told his story?

Becky: Yes, Tebow was the keynote speaker for the evening. As you know, he and his parents have a compelling story about his mother's decision not to terminate her pregnancy with Tim, even though doctors tried to persuade her to have an abortion.

Carole: What did he say in his talk or tell you directly that made you write such a strongly worded comment about his faith?

Becky: There were two things that really stuck out in my mind about Tebow's commitment to the Lord. First, he told the story of being approached by Focus on the Family to do the 2010 Super Bowl commercial. During the original meetings, he was warned that some endorsers might sever their relationships with him because of Tebow's association with Focus, a prolife, Christian organization. Well, the warning came true. Two endorsements immediately ended, but here's how Tebow responded. He simply told them, "Thank you." In other words, he showed the endorsers who turned away from him that he was not going to be influenced by their money.

The second thing was his reaction after being prayed for by a godly man attending the dinner. It's hard to put into words what I believe was in Tebow's heart. But when the "amen" was spoken, he looked up and wiped away tears. You could see in his eyes that his passion for Christ was greater than his passion for football. He even said in his message something like, "Football. It's a game. What does it really matter when it's all said and done?"

Carole: He wasn't putting down football . . . he was just trying to put the game into eternal perspective. I like that. How did his words seem to affect the crowd? How did they affect you?

Becky: Tebow's words were energizing to the crowd. There were lots of "amens" and rounds of applause. Grown men were crying and women were cheering. Remember, this fund-raising gala was in Texas, where football is king and Jesus is Lord!

I was most affected by the illustration of his final point: Finish strong. He shared that when he walked off the field after completing the game-winning pass for the 2009 BCS National Championship, his coach Urban Meyer grabbed him in a hug, pulled Tebow's head to his shoulder and said, "Attaboy! You did it. You finished strong."

But that's not where the story ends. As much as Tebow enjoyed hearing that from his coach, one day he longs to hear the same from his Lord. I will never forget that illustration.

Carole: Becky, you are one of my frequent workout partners, so I can attest to the fact that you are serious about maintaining physical fitness. Why do you think our health is important to God?

Becky: God has chosen to reside in the form of His Holy Spirit in the physical body of believers. Health is critical to believers, because the Spirit of God is worthy of a strong tabernacle. But since each of us is a four-sided individual, it is not just exercising and eating that I'm talking about here. This is what I love about First Place 4 Health. It helps me keep a balance on all four sides—physical, mental, emotional and spiritual.

Carole: I know you're a sports fan, because you and Johnny love to talk sports. I'm always amazed at the statistics you know.

Becky: Yeah, I love sports, especially college football and Southeast Conference football!

Carole: In this chapter of *Hope 4 You*—written just before the NFL draft picks will be announced—I predict that athletes like Tim Tebow, who are open about their faith in the Lord, will continue to serve Him, even when they become professional players and are paid what some may say are outrageous sums of money. What do you think of my prediction, now that you've met one who is a top draft choice?

Becky: This NFL draft class has three great college quarterbacks who are open about their love for the Lord. Not only do I believe that Tebow will carry the banner of Christ high and long during and following his NFL career, but Sam Bradford of Oklahoma and Colt McCoy of Texas will be doing the same.

The second story is close to my heart as a grandmother and demonstrates how faithful God is to provide the needs of those who work so diligently in His service. That can certainly be said about my daughter Lisa, an essential part of First Place 4 Health.

My Son's Miracle

By Lisa Lewis Cramer

When my son, Carl, was in sixth grade, he knew he wanted to play the guitar. For his birthday we decided to give him a basic (cheap) guitar and amp and pay for a few lessons to see if he liked it and would really practice. Carl seemed to love it, and I never once had to tell him to practice.

On week three of the lessons his teacher asked if he could speak to me alone. He told me he rarely got to teach a student like Carl. He not only had learned the three weekly chords the teacher assigned, but all the others on the assignment sheet. There were no more chords to teach him! His teacher was amazed.

In eighth grade, Carl was asked to play in the praise and worship band at school. Well, it didn't take long for Carl to figure out that his guitar was not exactly a fine-tuned instrument and that his amp was less than adequate. Around September, he began hinting that for Christmas it would really be great to have a "Fender Stratocaster" guitar. He said his dream preference would be an American-made Strat in the Sunburst pattern. He said he knew they were around $2,000, so if that was too expensive, he would be okay with a foreign-made "Fender" that was only around $800.

What Carl didn't know was that we were really cutting back due to a slow business year and that his entire Christmas would be around $200.

As a parent, there's nothing worse than having a child who wants just one certain gift, yet you know you can't supply that for him. I've always hated to pray for monetary items. I felt it was selfish when there were people in need of so much more than a silly guitar. I told Carl that he needed to pray about this one. I had only discussed this with my husband, and we were already planning on dealing with the disappointment on Christmas morning.

Well, for those of you who don't know, there is nothing my mom and dad like better than a good resale shop or garage sale. My mom's favorite hangout is the Goodwill store. My father also loves music.

So the first week of November, I got a phone call from my dad. It seems he'd come across a used guitar at a garage sale and wanted to know if Carl might want it. The seller told him it was a really good one worth $1,500 and in great shape. Well, me of little faith, the first thing I'm thinking is that Dad has been "had." He knew nothing about guitars. How was I going to tell him that my son only wanted a specific guitar, not a garage-sale model?

I decided to ask more about it anyway. He said the guy told him it was a Fender Stratocaster, made in America ("not a cheap foreign model"), and it was the Sunburst pattern . . . but my dad didn't know whether Carl would like that pattern.

After picking my chin up off the floor, I had to ask, "Daddy, what did you *pay* for that guitar?"

He said, "Well, I think I got a pretty good deal. I told him how much my grandson loves to play the guitar, and he sold it to me for $200 and even threw in the carrying case that's worth $165. But if Carl doesn't want it, I have a guy who will probably buy it for what I paid."

I was speechless. Never in my life had I witnessed a miracle worked out in every detail so perfectly. My earthly father was clueless to my son's one wish, but my heavenly Father had already taken care of it. My son still talks about that Christmas and says he'll never part with the guitar his grandpa found him. What a great impact it has made in his life to know that his heavenly Father orchestrated the entire thing on his behalf. I thank God that He is still a God of miracles, and His way is always better than anything I can imagine or plan.

For Study

1. Briefly tell what you do in your "day job" (whether it earns you a paycheck or not).

   ____
   ____
   ____
   ____
   ____

   List three things about your day job that you love and three things that you wish you could change.

   ____
   ____
   ____
   ____
   ____

2. Think of a person you know whose work habits, environment and relationships have an *intentionality* about them that you recognize to be that person's successful efforts to serve God through his or her day job. Describe what you have observed about this person, including an aspect of his or her behavior or attitude in the work environment that you could adopt into your own.

   ____
   ____
   ____
   ____
   ____

3. Describe how your job currently complements your desire to serve God in your work.

____
____
____
____
____

Describe an action you could take or an attitude you could adopt *tomorrow or next week* that would make your work habits, work environment and work relationships more successful in your desire to serve God.

____
____
____
____
____

Dear Lord, I want to serve You with my life, including my job. Show me how to accomplish this on a day-to-day basis. Help me understand that the work I do is important to Your kingdom on earth. I dedicate myself to doing my work with excellence and honor, because I represent You. Amen.

9

God's People Provide Hope

We also rejoice in our sufferings, because we know that suffering produces perseverance; perseverance, character; and character, hope.
ROMANS 5:3-4

I love what my friend Virelle Kidder writes in her autobiography, *The Best Life Ain't Easy, But It's Worth It:* "Authentic Christians exude the aroma of God's family love without trying. Familiar, yet hard to place at first, it's an aroma like company's coming, family fun, acceptance, mercy, and love all rolled into one. It smells of everything good and lovely, of freedom to grow, delicious warmth and laughter, music and beauty, grace and forgiveness.

"But part of the aroma is foreign to my senses, otherworldly. It's something I know little of, but am powerfully drawn to. It smells like sacrifice. It can only be the smell of heaven."[1]

This chapter's Scripture passage is followed by another key verse: "And hope does not disappoint us, because God has poured out his love into our hearts by the Holy Spirit, whom he has given us" (Rom. 5:5). I think the Holy Spirit living in the hearts of people who follow Christ is what provides that appealing fragrance that draws us to Christians, as Virelle describes. Is it a sweetness? Maybe. A boldness? Often. A gentleness? Usually. A passion? Always.

And yet, according to verses 3-4, suffering is also part of the Christian walk. Suffering produces perseverance. Perseverance produces character. And character produces hope. Isn't it wonderful how God moves His people through the process from suffering to hope?

I don't know of a single mature Christian who has not suffered, often mightily. In some cases (and I'll write of a few), they have experienced such extreme distress that non-Christians sometimes are puzzled by how they can keep smiling. In fact, many of the most dynamic, effective and inspiring people I know in the world of ministry—and here I'm including fellow writers, conference leaders and speakers, plus people who may form your traditional concept of "ministry," such as pastors—have suffered greatly, sometimes over and over.

These hope-filled people have not deluded themselves with a cross-less Christ; they know there is no hope without the cross. The cross defines the work of our Savior. I think we live in a time when many people are delusional about what it means to be a Christian. They want Jesus and all the good, easy parts of the walk, but not the dying. Following Jesus is more than going behind Him through some lovely meadow—it's embracing the cross, dying to self, living for Him.

Is your life filled with God's people? If not, you are missing out on one of the most inspiring paths to hope. The richness of their lives—the trauma and tragedy that God has led them through into triumph—will spill into your life as a testimony to the hope-filled life you, too, can experience.

The Canaanite Woman

A short but significant story is tucked into Matthew 15:21-28. It's about the Canaanite woman (she was a Gentile, or non-Jew). She approached Jesus when He was in an area that's now modern-day Lebanon. A shallow read of this story might leave you wondering if Jesus and His disciples were giving her the brush-off.

She cried out to Jesus, calling Him "Lord, Son of David" (v. 21). *So far so good*, you may think. Then she begs Him for mercy and says that her daughter is suffering terribly from demon possession. The next sentence is, "Jesus did not answer a word" (v. 23). His disciples pick up on this and urge Him, "Send her away, for she keeps crying out after us" (v. 23). *How cruel*, you may think, or maybe even, *How calloused*. That's followed by the words in red, Jesus' voice: "I was sent only to the lost sheep of Israel" (v. 24). Again, that sounds like a personal rejection unless you remember that Jesus knew the future—that what we now call the gospel would spread throughout the world.

Bless her heart—the Canaanite woman did not give up! She promptly knelt before Jesus and said, "Lord, help me!" (v. 25). He answered, "It is not right to take the children's bread and toss it to their dogs" (v. 26). He was making the point that His message was first for the Jews. But she dares to argue just a bit, pleading, "Yes, Lord . . . but even the dogs eat the crumbs that fall from their masters' table" (v. 27). In verse 28, Jesus answers, "Woman, you have great faith! Your request is granted." And her daughter was healed that very hour.

What I love about this exchange is exactly that: It's an exchange. The woman understood what Jesus was saying, but—rather than shrinking back—she pleaded with Him, using logic and passion. She was begging for help for her daughter, and she communicated to Jesus that she was willing to accept crumbs. He rewarded her faith.

In this exchange, Jesus also did the Canaanite woman a great service for her spiritual health; His response from beginning to end *strengthened her resolve*. To me this exchange is a template for how we can relate to our Lord—with honesty, passion and submission. Their exchange is a tiny window, because it's so brief, but it's there. Jesus *seems* to rebuff her. But in today's language, she steps up to the plate. Through their communication, they connect. No doubt He knows her heart, even while it almost seems like He's rebuffing her; but in reality He is pulling out of her a willingness deep inside herself to engage with Him, to trust her belief in Him, to submit to Him as an act of her faith.

Submission

Ah, the *S* word—"submission." Not the easiest thing to achieve. But people in the First Place 4 Health program mention over and over again that submission to the Lord is their first and most important step to a healthy lifestyle.

In fact, just understanding what submission means is actually the step before submitting. It means putting Him first. This goes beyond the act of beginning our day with prayer (although that's a good habit to develop). It means putting His priorities for our life before our priorities. Ironically, when we think about this, His priorities *are* our priorities—or they should be, if we're honest and if we understand how protective He is of what's in our best interest. But sometimes we dumb down this concept by thinking, *God says my body is His temple . . . so I need to lose weight . . . which means I shouldn't eat even a bite of ice cream.*

God is not a meanie! He *loves* us. Are we surrounding ourselves with people who know and understand this? If not, begin today. Encourage your children to begin today.

A nurse named Debbie attended a Boy Scout event where her son, Anthony, was playing the drums. Debbie was sitting in the audience with her daughter, Grace, who is Anthony's twin, when suddenly they noticed a boy about 15 years old wearing a cleverly worded T-shirt. The front read: *Virginity rocks!* On the back were these words: *I love my wife even though I haven't met her yet.*

Debbie and her husband, Bill, love the message of this shirt, because they teach their children to save sex for marriage and they are already praying for the spouses they trust God to send for Grace and Anthony. Like our Father God, they want what's best for their children. And they know the alarming statistics about the high failure rate for marriages between people who experience sexual intimacy while they are dating or even engaged. Debbie and Bill teach their twins to respect their own body and to respect the body of whomever they might date. This is an act of submission to God. It's also for the very practical reason that retaining an attitude of sexual purity increases the chances that Anthony and Grace will find their dates—and, ultimately, their mates—among people with the same values.

Redemption

Just like the subheadings of this chapter, redemption follows submission.

Depending on your church background, here are some words that may pop into your mind when you think of redemption: conversion, rebirth, atonement, absolution, remission of sin, expiation, propitiation. Maybe you think of redemption as compensation for a wrong, or balancing the scales of justice for a person's sin or wrongdoing, which Christians know to be Jesus' death on the cross, followed by His return in a resurrected body.

To be clear, I'm not a theologian. (I had to look up some of those words, too—okay, a lot of those words.) My point here is not word definitions. My point is to remind you that God's people have submitted to Him, and they are redeemed. That's why they have hope. They are not perfect, but they are *intentional* and *deliberate* about their resolve to trust Jesus and follow Him.

To be candid, their success may be less than ideal, because they are human. In this book you have read the stories of people who made bad choices—who kidded themselves about so many things that were essential to their life as a Christian. They ignored truths they should have been figuring out as they matured in their Christian walk, or maybe they considered themselves smarter than everyone else. Perhaps they thought their trust in Christ provided them with a magic invisible shield; but I've learned the hard way that Christians aren't invincible and that while miracles certainly happen in the Christian walk, magic does not.

Maybe they hadn't figured out that being a believer means seeking what is God's best for their life—or surrounding themselves with hope-filled people who are doing the same thing.

Bottom line: Maybe they didn't seek out wiser people than themselves.

The Rest of the Story . . .

Here's a truth about some of the people I invited to share their stories with you: God brought them through difficult, even tragic, circumstances, and now they've learned such valuable lessons that they tell their compelling stories to others. As stupid as their choices may have been, as tragic as the circumstances perpetrated upon them, they trusted God and became so strong that He can use them today.

Do you remember Mitchell from chapter 2, "Building a Fortress Around Hope"? He once was addicted to Internet porn, and his marriage and family life were in shambles. Today his marriage is solid, his family is loving and tight-knit, and he counsels regularly with men who have been through the same hell on earth, as he calls it—a good name for pornography online or any other kind, if you ask me.

Mitchell is one of God's people. He provides hope to others. As upsetting as it is to think of the bad things Mitchell did, I would rather know a person like him than someone who has not been forged in the fire, whose faith is lukewarm.

Kate, whose story was told in chapter 3, "Walking with God," is the woman who went through a divorce in which she lost everything she had brought into a marriage she entered when she was nearly 40 years old. She was only awarded one asset, a piece of real estate with a nice view of the water. She prayed that she would be able to make ends meet until the property reached a specific value, which was more than 50 percent above what it was worth when she prayed that prayer. The amount was on the advice of Christian people helping her to accomplish an important financial goal.

Guess what? God answered Kate's prayer. And He did so almost immediately, a miracle in itself, considering that an asset like real estate is subject to market value—a limitation in man's world, but not in God's world. And, as the late Paul Harvey would say, here's the rest of the story . . .

Kate told about God's miraculous solution through the couple who purchased her property. The wife happens to be a doctor of obstetrics and gynecology, treating pregnant women and delivering babies. After this OB/GYN heard Kate's story, she immediately became convicted of God's holiness. She realized that she must never again do a procedure in her medical practice that might result in taking the life of an unborn child. And she went public with her new attitude toward life; she told her medical practice partners, her patients, everyone who would listen!

In other words, as this OB/GYN explained to Kate, although she did not work in an abortion clinic, she occasionally did in-office procedures that she knew in advance would cause the death of a baby in its mother's womb. But, when she heard Kate's story, she recognized how real God is and how much He pays attention to people's attitudes and actions. Before that, this doctor had fooled herself into thinking that certain procedures were medically necessary—even that they were solutions for women with unwanted pregnancies. Now this physician was reversing her position and going public with it. Think how many unborn babies' lives have been spared!

Do you recall Jeremy, who told the story of his wife's infidelity, in chapter 6, "Forgiveness Restores Hope"? His forgiveness released Jennifer to a journey of such submission and redemption that she experienced a spiritual rebirth, complete with imagery in which God gave her a mental picture of herself as a baby with Him gazing lovingly on her and assuring her: "I am the lover of your soul."

Jennifer adds: "The Lord also supplied me with the image of Jesus as a warrior with a sword and armor. His eyes were fiery hot, and He told me, 'I am the defender of your soul.' It blew me away! Then I felt free, absolutely free. Suddenly, Scriptures enveloped me, reminding me that Jesus loves me wholeheartedly—a pure and wholesome love like the perfect love of a godly bridegroom for his precious bride. Before that, I had been so full of shame. Now people came up to me and asked, 'What just happened? Your face is absolutely glowing!' All this happened during an intense prayer service."

If people do not personally know the Lord, how can they know about God's transforming love unless His people tell their story and provide that hope?

Costly Discipleship

As I write this chapter, today's news includes an incredible story about two of God's faithful people. I must warn you: This is not for the squeamish, but here is a synopsis.

A Christian couple in Pakistan refused to convert to Islam. With the help of police, Muslim *extremists* (I emphasize "extremists," because I know the majority of Muslims would be horrified by this act) set the husband on fire and raped his wife. The incident occurred in front of a local police station. The couple's three children, ranging in age from 7 to 12, were forced to watch their parents being brutalized.

I share this shocking story to remind you that God's people sometimes suffer for His sake. Put another way, some are persecuted because of their resolute belief that Jesus is their Savior.

Another truth that's hard to accept is that even God's most vocal followers are not immune to heart-breaking losses. I'm thinking here of Stephen Curtis Chapman, Christian songwriter and singer, whose daughter died in the driveway when her brother accidentally backed up the family vehicle, crushing her fragile body.

Out of this tragedy came a message of enormous hope. The Chapmans had prayed that God would let them *see* a sign confirming what they believed about God's goodness, as they were holding on to that belief so desperately in their time of grief. God's answer to this prayer is incredible.

They found a picture that Maria Sue had drawn of a six-petal flower with only one petal colored in. The Chapmans had six children, and now one was in heaven—or "complete in her journey into God's presence," as the family understood this drawing, which was the girl's last one before her death.

Also, she had written the word "see" on the back, a word the five-year-old had never written before. God had answered this very personal prayer even before the Chapmans prayed it, even before the Chapmans *needed* to pray it. And God gave this answer to an entertainer with a huge following, one who would surely share this story.

As this chapter's verse reminds us, "Suffering produces perseverance; perseverance, character; and character, hope" (Rom. 5:3-4).

God, as the perfect parent, takes us through our suffering and entrusts us with the message of hope to share with others.

More Real-life Stories

My own children are inspirations to me. All three trusted Christ as their Savior when they were young, and they grew in their faith as adults. When Shari was killed by a drunk driver, her two siblings were understandably shaken by this tragic and life-changing event for all of us. I'm proud to say, however, that their faith—and sense of hope—remained intact. Here's what my son, John Lewis, and his sister Lisa Cramer wrote to share with you.

Shari Symank, My Sister

By John Lewis

I got the call from my mom on Thanksgiving night, 2001. I was standing in the kitchen, and the TV was on and the kids were talking, and I had to step out into the backyard, because I knew I couldn't have heard her right.

She said, "Shari has been in an accident, and it doesn't look good." All I could feel was disbelief. It just couldn't be happening. She was saying things like "her leg was cut off" and "they were leaving Jeff's parent's house." But it just didn't compute.

When I arrived, the ambulance had taken Shari to the hospital, so I drove Jeff and their kids there myself. I felt like I had to get us to the hospital as quickly as I could, as if that would make a difference. And Jeff looked over at me and said, "John, you don't have to hurry." Those words just pierced my heart, because I knew what they meant.

When we arrived at the hospital, Shari was still in surgery. The overriding feeling for me was still disbelief. Things like this just don't happen to people you know and love. I knew the doctors were going to fix her.

It wasn't long before they came out and told us the heartbreaking news. Shari was gone.

It still seems like just yesterday. I sometimes wonder what might be different today if she were still alive.

Shari, My Sister and Best Friend

By Lisa Lewis Cramer

We were at my husband's grandparents' farm that Thanksgiving night. I began praying as soon as we got in the car to drive home. I'd been told her leg was severed, so I knew how serious it was.

But I was so sure we could get through this. I was already thinking about her rehab and how I would help her with that. It was an incredible shock when I learned she was gone.

Jeff and all three girls lived with us afterward. It was such a sweet time . . . but difficult emotionally, of course.

Shari and I weren't just sisters; we were best friends. We married within six months of each other, me first. Then as newlyweds we lived side by side in cheap little rent houses, both couples helping each other get by. Shari and I would shop together, spending time at the mall not only to enjoy each other's company but also to enjoy the mall's air conditioning! I'm super organized, and she was incredibly creative. Our idea of an evening together was me cleaning out a closet while she sewed curtains.

It's still hard to believe. Even now, when something happens, I think, *Oh, I've got to tell Shari.*

For Study

1. Consider what is your concept of the lifestyles, circumstances and personalities of God's people. Do you think they all live charmed lives, without grief or sorrow? Does crabgrass ever grow in the yards of Christians? Worse, does tragedy ever strike their lives? Do you think they are all sweetness and kindness, never losing their temper or feeling down? Take a few moments to picture in your mind a Christ follower who is mature and filled with hope but who you happen to know has suffered greatly. Describe that person's walk with the Lord in the spaces below—how God has allowed suffering to produce perseverance, how perseverance has produced character and how character has produced hope. Be sure to include the lessons you

have learned about life from this person and what personal qualities ("aroma") draw you to him or her.

____

____

____

____

2. What hardship has God allowed you to experience that has strengthened you? Describe the circumstance and the process He led you through that give you hope.

____

____

____

____

3. Consider what is your concept of being one of God's people. Do you think it means living on the other side of the globe in a jungle where people need to hear about Christ's love and sacrifice (and from people you consider more qualified than you to tell about it)? Or do you think you could be one of God's people without ever leaving your ZIP or postal code? List three ways you can be active in the near future as one of God's people providing hope.

____

____

____

____

Thank You, God, for bringing Your strong and vibrant people into my life to provide hope. Forgive me for bitterness that I may have clung to when bad experiences occurred in my life. Help me to see how these very circumstances are opportunities for me to grow into the likeness of Your Son, Jesus, who suffered greatly on my behalf. Show me how to embrace the life You want for me, which naturally includes suffering, perseverance, character-building and the greatest measure of hope. Amen.

10

God's Word Prescribes Hope

Through endurance and the encouragement of the Scriptures we might have hope.
ROMANS 15:4

Remember Colt McCoy, Sam Bradford and Tim Tebow from chapter 8, "Working with God"? As I write today, the gridiron futures of these outstanding college quarterbacks have been sealed by the NFL draft system. McCoy was selected by the Cleveland Browns, Bradford will play for the St. Louis Rams, and Tebow was drafted by the Denver Broncos.

I see a parallel between the NFL draft system and how Jesus selected His disciples: He was not looking for benchwarmers. He wanted people with raw talent who were teachable. And He had the patience and, often, the directness of a coach.

Read the story in Matthew 17:14-23 where Jesus healed a boy who had seizures. This scene reminds me of how college quarterbacks move from their senior year to their rookie year with the pros. First, let's review a bit.

The scene with the demon-possessed boy opens right after one of the most spectacular events in the Bible—the Transfiguration (see Matt. 17:1-13). Jesus had taken Peter, James and John (the brother of James) to a mountaintop. Jesus' appearance changes right before their eyes: "His face shone like the sun, and his clothes became as white as the light" (v. 2). Then, just as suddenly, Jesus is joined by Moses and Elijah! And the story gets better. They hear the voice of God: "This is my Son, whom I love; with him I am well pleased. Listen to him!" (v. 5).

Within moments the disciples have experienced God's personal declaration that Jesus is His beloved Son and His instruction to listen to Jesus; plus they've seen and recognized two people who have been dead for centuries (my, how being in the presence of God clarifies things for us, doesn't it?).

Jesus' Quarterback

So what does Peter, Jesus' quarterback, do? He babbles nervously. First, he states, "Lord, it is good for us to be here." (I should control my sense of humor. I have an image of James and John turning to Peter at this point and saying, "Duh!")

Then Peter makes an offer to build shelters for all three—Jesus, Moses and Elijah. (Peter, so impetuous, is eager to *do something*. Just *being somewhere* is not his favorite sport.)

We learn in the remainder of the Transfiguration passage that the disciples fall facedown and then feel the touch of Jesus, who is now alone. As they descend the mountain together, Jesus asks them to keep to themselves what they've experienced. He and the disciples then discuss the role of John the Baptist.

Back down from the mountain, they come to a crowd where a man approaches Jesus, kneels before Him and requests that Jesus heal his son of seizures. The father reports that he had already requested the disciples to do this healing, but they had failed.

This is the point in the ongoing story where Jesus reminds me of a coach. At first He seems frustrated, but in the verses that follow we begin to understand what Jesus already knows. The disciples aren't ready for the work they eventually will do so capably—even heroically—after His death and resurrection.

At this point, they are rookies. They've been drafted to His team, and they think they can play. They have insights, but they haven't been inspired. Sure, they've seen Jesus perform miracles. They've heard His stories and stirring words. But now is their practice season, their warm-up. Yet they aren't really benchwarmers. Jesus did not choose benchwarmers! As the greatest coach, He wanted players who were chomping at the bit, eager to charge onto the field.

The Truth of God's Word

Does the Bible come alive when you read it? Do you see your life circumstances in it? Your life answers? Your hope?

If you think of First Place 4 Health only as a program that encourages nutritious food planning and healthful exercise, you're not seeing the Big Picture. You're missing God's perfect plan for you as players on His mission field. He made us—in His image—each as a highly individual human being with a body, mind, heart and soul.

Like rookie quarterbacks, we have to learn His ways. That involves more than the physical (strengthening, controlling, improving our throwing arm). It involves ongoing inspiration within our heart, mind and soul—preparing ourselves emotionally, mentally and spiritually as well as physically. One way we develop this is by reading the Bible on a regular basis, using insights from scholars and from wise people we know, meditating on its truths, applying them to our lives.

Are you a new Christian who's not in the habit of studying the Bible? If so, you may feel overwhelmed by its length and seeming complexity. I encourage you to begin a study—hopefully in the company of other believers.

Have you been following Christ and studying the Bible for years? Then you know that the deeper you go into God's Word, the deeper it gets. We can never completely plumb its depths in our lifetime on earth. But we can try. And as we read and study, His Big Picture—God's playbook, if you will—is revealed to us more and more and with greater clarity.

Yes, we may chuckle at Peter, fumbling a bit. We feel compassion for him too. At Peter's point in God's story—which is what the Bible is—he cannot yet see all that's in store for him, nor for all of God's people who will follow. Neither can we, which is why we empathize with Peter and why we must continue to delve into the truths of God's Word with wonder and expectation. Because if we do, we will grow, we will learn, we will come to understand how God's story applies to us.

The Bible appears daunting. It's lengthy; it's complicated. (I sometimes think if the Bible weren't challenging, we humans might not find it so fascinating and, frankly, fun.)

The Bible is also simple. Its overarching truth is that *God is determined to give to His people what they don't deserve.* In each of the many generations covered in God's story, which spans thousands of years, the people receive a glimpse of God's goodness and grace. They experience Him as the perfect parent—caring for them, admonishing them when they fail, helping them to survive even when their circumstances seem hopeless. Yet they do have hope—in Him.

God's Perfect Prescription

When I chose the verb "prescribes" for the chapter title, "God's Word Prescribes Hope," I was thinking of a doctor's prescription pad. On it the doctor writes exactly what we need to heal.

In First Place 4 Health, we see so many people who have self-inflicted health problems. They worry constantly. They handle this by overeating. They work too hard. They lack proper exercise. They harbor grudges. They lose self-esteem. They fail to love—others *and* themselves.

Meantime, along with their weight, their blood pressure rises. So does their cholesterol. Their back hurts. Their knees ache. And, alone, they cannot end their unhealthy cycle.

Do you see how unhealthy behaviors and attitudes affect the whole person--our bodies, our emotions, our feelings, our spirits?

These people with their often self-imposed health problems become lonely . . . frustrated . . . angry. They blame others. They blame themselves. They may even blame God.

But God, the perfect physician, has a prescription, a solution; and it's even in writing. It's His Word(s) to us, the Bible. When we read it, we learn how to live. We learn that much of our personal stress—and resulting bad health—is self-inflicted. We learn over and over that God is providing us with the love and care we need. What's more, He is pursuing us with it, determined that we have every chance to accept it.

It's true that part of His guidance is to teach us that our actions have consequences. If we live on sweets, we'll grow fat. If we choose not to forgive, we'll become bitter. Yet, He's also eager to provide us with a clear path to success. You might say He's easier on us than we are on ourselves, if our doctors' reports are any indication.

In short, His story, which can be our story, shows His absolute determination to provide us what we don't deserve, to reverse the damage we have done to ourselves, to rescue us from ourselves. Now that is hope!

God Leads Me to James 1:2-4

I am in the habit of rising early, often through a prompting from the Lord. The early morning hours (some would call these middle-of-the-night hours) are special times for me to spend with Him, especially in His Word.

On the morning that was to be my daughter Shari's last day on earth, Thanksgiving Day, I woke up at 4 A.M. It was tempting just to turn over and try to go back to sleep. But on this day—which would turn out to be the most devastating one of my life—God wouldn't let me stay in bed. I sensed an urgency to get up and turn to the book of James.

While the coffee was brewing, I opened my Bible to a familiar passage: "Consider it pure joy, my brothers, whenever you face trials of many kinds, because you know that the testing of your faith develops perseverance. Perseverance must finish its work so that you may be mature and complete, not lacking anything" (Jas. 1:2-4).

God knew how that terrible day would unfold. He was preparing me even before it happened by drawing me to Scripture that would comfort and remind me that Jesus was already grieving with me, hours before the drunk driver would hit our daughter in plain sight of her loving husband, daughters and Jeff's parents and siblings.

God's Word is far more than a book. It is a miracle we see over and over again. Each verse fits together intricately, even though the entirety of the Bible was written over a period of centuries. God leads us to passages that will be meaningful to us—sometimes even before we need them.

Months after the accident that took my daughter's life, I was still in the book of James, because the experience in those early morning hours was so precious to me—and because James continued to minister to me day after day.

Another Real-life Story

Linda Askin shares how Psalm 118:24 came alive for her:

> "This is the day the LORD has made; let us rejoice and be glad in it" (Ps. 118:24). That familiar verse has had a new, fresh meaning for me since Valentine's Day 2010. On Sunday, the Lord's Day, Dutch's and my favorite day of the week, we awakened to a beautiful clear morning. The past weeks had been cold, wet and dreary, which perhaps was another reason the morning seemed so bright. "What would you like to have for breakfast today?" I asked him. "You know, I think I'd like two pancakes and scrambled eggs," he replied. After preparing his breakfast, I went into the bedroom to help him to the table. He had been home only two weeks from an eight-week stay at the hospital and rehabilitation, and it seemed that he was not getting any stronger. He ate his breakfast with great gusto and even commented, "This is so good!" It's funny, but I don't remember what the conversation was about while we ate. I just know it was a sweet time together.
>
> Removing the plates from the table to the kitchen, I noticed that Dutch had reached for his glass of water, taken a sip and began to choke. As we had done in the past, I encouraged him to talk to me to get air through his throat. "Dutch, Dutch, talk to me," I said. "Okay, okay," he whispered in a raspy voice.
>
> "It's Valentine's Day, Dutch. How much do you love me?" I asked. He replied, "I love you sooo much." Trying to keep him talking, I began to quote a Scripture that we often said together at the beginning or end of the day.

"This is the day the Lord has made . . ." then I noticed his arm gently moved to his side. He looked into my eyes with an incredible stare, and I knew. I knew at that moment we had a visitor. An angel had entered the room and taken Dutch right into the presence of our Lord, to his new eternal home. It's hard to fathom, but at that moment I was calm and felt joy. I felt the presence of the Lord in the very room that day. How can this be? The man I loved for 31 years!

Pondering the events of the past weeks, I now see and understand that God, in His wisdom, was preparing Dutch and me for the most unbearable, unthinkable separation, in a magnificent way.

The previous weeks had been extremely stressful because Dutch had been plagued with diarrhea due to long-term antibiotics. His body weakened so that getting out of a chair was monumental. I was facing decisions regarding what provision would be the best care for him. Should I resign my job that provided necessary funds to maintain our home? Should I hire someone to come into the home, which would also use up our income? I had discussed with Dutch seeing an attorney, and he agreed that I should meet with him to talk about the possibility of Medicaid and a nursing home.

My heart began to feel heavy—it seemed to weigh 5,000 pounds. The only place I could go for help, once again, was to the Lord. My plea was for discernment, wisdom and clarity to make the right decisions within the upcoming week, a feeling of urgency that time was short and a decision had to be made. The burden became heavier, because I had learned from Dutch, when he told me about his growing-up years, that—as it seemed to me—he'd lost or been abandoned by everyone he loved. As a child, he'd been in a body cast for several years, sent away from his family, then lived with his Aunt Mary. At the age of 10, his brother, to whom he was very close, died from a ruptured appendix. Several months after the death of his brother, his father was in a tractor accident and died three months later. His mother, a homemaker, had a nervous breakdown and took his sister to another state. Dutch was taken to an orphanage where he spent a year before his Aunt Mary came and got him. He had lived with her about a year when his uncle committed suicide.

At the age of 14, he was on his own and, with a friend, ended up in Phoenix. He was there a couple of years when he received a call from his sister that the family was reuniting in San Antonio. He managed to stay in school all those years and finished high school in San Antonio where he attended business college. After marriage and moving to Houston, he had a successful career in the oil business and traveled to Europe and Saudi Arabia.

Upon returning home after an extended trip, Dutch recalled that his wife said, "You do not live here anymore." They separated and divorced.

Then the Lord placed Dutch in my life at just the right time, and we meshed together like two peas in a pod. We enjoyed our church family, loved the same music and had many adventures together.

When he became ill, our season had changed, and I began to understand the term "long-suffering" up close and personal. The decisions to be made about his care seemed unthinkable, including the possibility of a nursing home, and I had feelings of guilt that I would be abandoning him too.

Then Saturday, February 13, arrived. The only thing scheduled was an appointment with an agency caregiver at 9:30 A.M. I'd made the appointment in preparation for returning to work, knowing that Dutch would need someone to care for him while I was away. Ron, a handsome young man, arrived right on time. After a time of getting acquainted, I asked if he would help shower Dutch and get him dressed. He said he would be more than happy to help.

I had a total peace that Dutch would be cared for in a gentle, special way. Ron left and I asked Dutch if he thought it would be okay if we "adopted" Ron.

The rest of the day was quiet and relaxed, mostly watching the Winter Olympics on TV. My friend Deborah arrived in the late afternoon to help with some problems I was having with my new computer. I invited Deborah to share our dinner. She accepted, and the three of us laughed about having Sunday dinner on Saturday night. Dutch asked Deborah about her girls, how they were doing in school and where her oldest would be going to college. The rest of the evening we spent watching the Olympics.

After retiring for bed, I was awakened in the night. I looked at Dutch, and I recall thinking that he was resting more peacefully than usual. The next thing I remember, it was morning. I went straight to the kitchen for my usual cup of coffee and remembered . . . it's Valentine's Day.

As I write, it has been about six weeks since that day. My thoughts about these events have come to mind almost every day since. In the most detailed way, God was preparing my heart for Dutch's homegoing. The weight of the previous week had been paralyzing. But on Saturday my heart was peaceful in a sweet connection of just being together as we went through the day. God, with the precision of a surgeon, prepared my mind and heart, and then the Great Surgeon began to cut away at my guilt, anger, frustration and heartache. A dear friend suggested that Ron, the young man who attended Dutch on Saturday, may have been an angel preparing Dutch for his homegoing as well.

Dutch's generosity was beyond anything I had ever known. As the minister who had known him well recalled at Dutch's memorial service, "He left this world with nothing else to give." While going through his personal effects, it became evident that that was true. His only real treasures were his books, and he freely gave those away or traded with other book lovers. His work was finished; truly he had nothing else to give.

Did I mention that Dutch brought absolute joy to many people through his faith, joy and encouragement? He did! During 31 years of marriage, I cannot recall an unkind word toward me or anyone else. He made us all laugh. And he gave us great joy and taught us, by example, how to love.

Today, God has given my heart sweet treasures of peace and, yes, joy! For "this is the day the LORD has made" (Ps. 118:24).

May I invite you also to rejoice and be glad in it?

For Study

1. Fill in the missing words from the Bible verse at the beginning of this chapter:

   "Through ________________ and the encouragement of the ________________ we might have ________________" (Rom. 15:4).

2. Describe your history of studying the Bible. Has it been on a regular basis? Has it been easy for you to accomplish? Difficult? Have you studied with a group of believers or sought guidance from scholars or people with more biblical wisdom than yours?

   ____

   ____

   ____

   ____

   ____

   ____

   ____

If your methods of studying God's Word seem inadequate, describe how you plan to step up your efforts. List several ways.

3. Update your hope meter at this point in your reading of *Hope 4 You* as you commit to studying or increasing the effectiveness of your study of God's Word. Jot notes about why the needle on your hope meter may have changed from the last time you updated it in this book.

Today I commit to studying Your Word, dear Lord.
I know it holds the truth for my life. I know that I cannot improve my health in all four areas—the physical, mental, emotional and spiritual—without learning more about what You have written and preserved in Your story.
Please help me to make it become my story. Amen.

11

Waiting on God

But those who hope in the LORD *will renew their strength.*
They will soar on wings like eagles; they will run and not grow weary,
they will walk and not be faint.
ISAIAH 40:31

Since the beginning of this book, I've made two big moves—into a new home and into a new office setup. Both were exhausting experiences, but God's hand was with us at every step (even while we gutted a Houston townhouse to custom-build it so Johnny won't need to climb stairs). It's wonderful to be in a new home that's truly ours. I feel that I can bring the Hurricane Ike chapter of my life to a close.

For weeks I'd been driving by what was to become the new office location, sensing God's tug. He always knows my needs. My drive time became prayer time. *Is this where we should move the headquarters of First Place 4 Health? It's Your ministry, Lord, not mine.* He answered the prayer, and with confidence I signed the lease.

Waiting for the end of projects, like moving to a new office location and building a house, takes patience, sometimes more than I seem to have.

Waiting can be agonizing. It also can be a time of preparation. It requires patience and often perseverance. Waiting on God is part of God's plan for His people. He wants us to soar like eagles.

Sometimes waiting is just that—"waiting," what soldiers jokingly call "hurry up and wait." But much of their career is nothing to laugh about. We all know stories of families waiting for their warrior loved ones to return from the battlefronts in Iraq and

Afghanistan. Fortunately, the overwhelming majority of these brave men and women come home. Sadly, some military families wait for years for closure regarding family members who did not survive. I read about a woman who finally laid to rest the remains of her husband who was shot down over Laos . . . 38 years ago.

Sometimes waiting prepares us. We know of families who have endured long waits, even years, for an adoption to come through. And waiting for God's miracle of a pregnancy can seem to take an eternity for couples eager to conceive. Yet I know of no one that has waited for a child who then dwells on the agony of the wait after they welcome the precious baby into their family. Most see God's purpose for the waiting—an opportunity to turn to Him in prayer, a reminder that He's always their source of hope. I look forward to sharing a real-life story to demonstrate this—one that's close to my heart as a grandmother.

Patience Versus Perseverance

Sometimes waiting means exercising perseverance, holding back our own desires so that God can work through us. It means exercising an even higher level of patience because what we're waiting for is so close at hand. I'm thinking here of situations where people who trust Christ as their Savior have family members who are not believers. In a few pages you will meet a woman whose husband was trained and employed as a pastor, but he has turned away from the Lord. Yet she has hope!

Often we wait for a family member to see a truth that we can see so clearly because of our love and our prayers for his or her wellbeing. Maybe as the parent of a single man or woman, we're praying for a potential spouse to come into the picture when less worthy prospects have come and gone. This is perseverance! We don't want our children to experience heartache, which is inevitable in breakups, yet we don't want them to cling to people they care about when they haven't matured enough to make a good marriage decision. I'll be sharing another story about this that's close to my heart as a grandmother.

Waiting that requires perseverance can be times when we're directly opposed by the enemy. Or we're working fiercely to hold back on our own desires so that God can work through us. Sometimes it even means we're fighting our own sinful natures. But we know the effort will be worth it because of the lessons we'll learn and the strength we'll gain in the process. Don't miss my interview in this chapter with a woman who writes and speaks on sexual healing. She's an authority on this issue, and her comments are amazing.

David and Bathsheba

Inappropriate sexual contact is always disappointing—even shocking—when we learn that it involves leaders, people we trust for good judgment, people we think should know how to wait on God for His best plan for every aspect of their lives, including sexual intimacy.

We only need to look directly in the Bible to find an example that confounds and confuses many. I'm thinking of the story of King David and Bathsheba, told in 2 Samuel 11. They committed the sin of adultery. Yet David's story shows how God takes people back into His fold when they confess their sins and seek His face once more.

Have you given any thought to the fact that we don't know much about Bathsheba, the woman with whom King David had the affair? We know she was married and that her husband was Uriah, a trusted soldier in the king's army. (We learn just how trustworthy and loyal Uriah is to his king in verses 11-17. When Operation Cover-up gets underway, my name for David's method of "handling" the fact that he has made Uriah's wife pregnant, Uriah winds up delivering his own death warrant!)

In those few verses leading up to the affair, we have no idea if Bathsheba realized the king was watching as she did her ritual bath. If she noticed him, did she cover herself? Or did she flaunt her assets? Did she demurely look away? Or did she bat her eyelashes at him?

Maybe there's a reason the author leaves us wondering and tells the story from David's point of view. David, a great and mighty king, was 100 percent responsible for his choices, no matter whether Bathsheba flirted or not. He was the leader who publicly confessed his faith in God and built his kingdom on God's promises.

Regardless of Bathsheba's actions, the king should have done the right thing. As Christ followers, so must we.

More Real-life Stories

My first story comes from daughter-in-law Lisa. Don't be surprised. I told you it would be a "grandmother story."

Pregnancy Prayer

By Lisa Lewis

When our oldest child was about four, we decided we wanted to have another baby. It didn't take long before I was pregnant. I was so excited.

At about six weeks, I started having severe pain on my right side. After several days of the pain getting worse, plus other symptoms, I went to the doctor and learned the pregnancy was ectopic. I lost that child and was heartbroken.

It wasn't long before I was pregnant again and everything seemed fine. Then at about six weeks, I miscarried.

I started to lose hope that we would be able to have any more children.

Surgeries during these two pregnancies reduced my chance of getting pregnant by 50 percent. However, 50 percent is plenty for God, and I got pregnant again!

I was considered high risk at this point, so I went to the doctor at six weeks. They used a device that would enable us to hear the baby's heartbeat. The nurse tried for about five minutes, but we were not able to hear the baby. The nurse left the room and got the doctor. He came in and couldn't find a heartbeat either. Then he told me that, based on the level of pregnancy hormone in my blood tests, we should hear the heartbeat by now.

It was late on Friday, so he recommended I go home and return Monday so we could try again with an ultrasound. I don't know how I answered him or paid my bill or made my way to my car.

A few minutes later, I was sitting alone in my car, sobbing. How was I going to sit at home all weekend thinking my baby had died? After sitting there for a while and crying, I said to myself, *Well, how dumb is this? Lisa, what are you doing? This is too big for you. Why don't you trust God with this? Give it to Him and let it go.*

So I started praying. As I prayed, the peace that came over me is indescribable. I drove home. I made it through the weekend fine. And when I went back to the doctor on Monday, I saw my beautiful little boy's heart beating on the sonogram. My little boy is now 6′1″, 195 pounds! My hope meter was at an all-time low for a little while, but when I trusted God, He filled it back up and then blessed me in a big way with a healthy child.

Nancy Sebastian Meyer has a speaking and writing ministry that's a great encouragement to people whose spouses aren't believers or have turned away from the Lord, as Nancy's husband has done. She's a role model for learning to wait on God. Here's my interview with this incredible woman, a member of First Place 4 Health:

Carole: Nancy, I love the name of your ministry—*hope4hearts*! Tell how you "hand out hope," as your website says.

Nancy: In 30 years of ministry to women, I've learned that the greatest balm for a battered soul is "hope." As God continues to make hope abound in my own life amidst myriad challenges, He equips me to share hope with others by being real, relevant and radiant.

Carole: You know a thing or two (or three) about waiting on God, the title of this chapter in *Hope 4 You*. You are quite open about the fact that your husband, Rich, is a former-pastor-turned-agnostic. Can you share with us the story behind this transition?

Nancy: After Rich and I graduated from Bible college and got married, he became a youth pastor, serving in two churches, each for two years. Although I did not see it at the time, Rich was becoming more and more disenchanted with ministry. As hindsight is clearer, I now believe he did all the right things in youth work, but he did them for God instead of with God. Without a strong relationship with God, all the things he did fell short. He eventually left church work for a secular job. Then shortly after our daughter was born, he completely defected on his faith and began calling himself an agnostic. I was shocked. Then came denial, blame and shame . . . and our marriage began to seriously deteriorate.

At the end of myself, I went to our pastor of counseling and came to the realization that even if I couldn't change Rich, I could work on me. And the changes God made in my life impacted Rich so profoundly that our love for each other returned—even the sex and romance! While it may sound like a romance novel with a happy ending, I can assure you that living with a self-proclaimed agnostic who fights off the Holy Spirit every single day is not a fun place to live. But through the ups and downs, zigs and zags of the past 19 years of Rich's defection from the faith, God has been faithful to me and to our family.

Carole: Do you mind sharing how this affects you as his wife?

Nancy: I've learned so many significant spiritual and life lessons over the years. Everything God writes in His Word about how to be a godly wife is true! And I keep learning and relearning as I walk this journey in step with the Spirit. If you were to look at my life as a bride and compare it with me today, you would—as I do—marvel at the patience, selflessness, faithfulness and 1 Corinthians 13 type of love God continues to grow in me. But I have not arrived—nor do I expect perfection until I see my Lord face to face. In the meantime, He sustains me with peace, comfort and joy!

Carole: What is your prayer for Rich, and what have you learned from this experience about the process of waiting on God?

Nancy: God is God. God is faithful to His Word, His promises and His character. God is omnipresent and sovereign, which means He has gone before us and nothing ever surprises Him—He's prepared and makes sure that I am. I can trust Him in all things, all the time. His ways of doing things and His way of thinking about things are *so not me*—and I'm learning to look to Him and ask Him before I try it my way . . . most times! *Patience, Nancy,* I tell myself. God is working even when you can't see Him. Try looking somewhere else. Where is He working? What is He doing? Look to Jesus!

Carole: What is your best advice to women and men whose spouses don't share a faith in God?

Nancy: Don't do life alone! Find God-believing friends who will be real encouragers. An encourager comes in two forms: an arm around the shoulders and a kick in the pants! We need both to remind us to look to Jesus, and to sometimes point Him out when we cannot see.

I promised you another story that's close to my heart as a grandmother. It's by my daughter . . .

A New Beginning

By Lisa Lewis Cramer

Several years ago my neighbors and I had a weekly prayer group. Six or seven moms met Friday mornings to pray for our kids' needs, college exams, weddings, births of grandchildren and other life issues. The salvation of one of these dear ladies was something only God could have orchestrated.

During this time my daughter had been dating a boy she'd met in high school. He was a nice enough guy, but I knew, as only moms do, that it was not a healthy relationship. I also knew that she'd "settled" and was just "comfortable" with him and her life at that time. She was attending junior college in town, had no real career goals and below average grades. I also knew that only God could change the situation. After praying for a year that God would just make this boy go away, my wonderful neighbor, Fay, suggested we pray instead that He might send a godly young man into her life to show Katherine her true worth as the daughter of the King.

Two months later Katherine attended a birthday party and met the young man she's now dated for three years. He's a Christian of godly character, trustworthy and has just finished his master's at Texas A&M. All I prayed for was a godly young man for my daughter. God gave that to Katherine; but what she also received was a new ambition to get her grades up so she could go off to college. She has now graduated from Texas A&M with a major in horticulture and a minor in business. She was given a whole new outlook on life. The craziest part is that this boy has lived three doors down from us for 11 years. They love to say how the verse "love thy neighbor" has taken on a whole new meaning.

Another First Place 4 Health member is Barbara Wilson, book author and speaker on the subject of sexual healing. She has fascinating new scientific information about the tragic results to our psyche and our physical selves caused by inappropriate sexual behavior, such as sex outside the bonds of marriage. She was invited as a speaker to the United Nations Summit 2010, a conference on the Status of Women. Here's my interview:

Carole: Barbara, your website begins with these bold words: "You've had sex . . . and now sex has you." Could you elaborate?

Barbara: When God said that "two becomes one," He was talking about a bond that happens through the sexual union between husband and wife that's not only physical, but spiritual, emotional and even chemical. Recent science has confirmed this bond by showing how men and women release a hormone called oxytocin that is God's super-human glue, causing an exclusive attachment or bond, and in fact giving us, as scientists explain, a permanent imprint on the brain of each other.

When we save sex for the one we spend our lives with, this bond is reinforced throughout marriage, strengthening the bond into a deep, loving attachment. But in our culture many people are having premarital sex with multiple partners, and science now shows that with each successive partner we actually release less oxytocin, inhibiting our ability to bond. And then we get married, thinking the past is all wiped away; but in reality we've brought all those past partners with us chemically, spiritually, emotionally and physically. Once we have sex it now has a hold on us . . . attaching us permanently to every partner we've had sex with.

Carole: Wow, I've never heard of oxytocin or the science that supports why God's plan is for each of us to have one sexual partner—His plan of saving sexual intimacy for marriage. Readers of *Hope 4 You* may be like me, wanting to read more about this scientific research and its results. What do you recommend?

Barbara: I have several resources I share with listeners when I speak on this topic, many referenced in my books. I suggest you start by reading *Hooked: New Science on How Casual Sex Is Affecting Our Children* by Joe S. McIlhaney, Jr., MD and Freda McKissic Bush, MD.

Carole: You write that "just sex means your body, soul, mind and spirit have become one with another." As a First Place 4 Health participant, you know that we address the importance of good health in those four areas. Why do you think God is concerned about our health?

Barbara: God has created us as whole beings, and that means our body, soul and mind interconnect in every area of our life. When we misuse any one area, it affects all the others.

Let's just discuss the sexual area for a moment. When we misuse God's design for sex, the wounding goes beyond just the physical, because the union includes all those parts. The world would have us believe that sex is just physical. But in fact, God says it involves a total union of body, soul and mind. This is why there needs to be healing for a sexual past as well as forgiveness.

I'm convinced God has given us all we need to have health in every area of our lives, and He wants us to seek Him for wholeness and freedom in all these areas. I find that when one of these areas is suffering, it affects all the others. When I'm not taking care of my physical health, such as eating healthy and exercising, it seeps into my emotional life as well. The same goes for my spiritual life. When I'm not nurturing this area, it makes me lazy in the other areas as well.

Carole: Do you mind sharing how God called you to this line of work for ministry?

Barbara: I can assure you I never dreamed of growing up to speak and write on sexual healing . . . that's for sure! It's certainly something God has called me to because of my own past.

I was born and raised into a Christian home; my dad was a Baptist pastor. I gave my heart to Jesus when I was seven years old, and I planned to serve Him with my whole life . . . I was even willing to go to Africa! But when I went away to a Christian high school for my senior year, I was unprepared for the sexual temptations I'd face, since no one in my generation talked about sex—not the church, our parents, school. So, thinking that as a Christian I wouldn't struggle with this, I was caught unaware when I fell in love for the first time with a young man I planned to marry. After several months of making out we eventually had sex, although I'd always planned to wait until marriage. That was very shameful for me, and I suffered greatly from the regret. That led us to elope, because my parents were unsupportive of our union. We were young, and the marriage didn't last, so I found myself back at home, falling again into the same temptation until finally I got pregnant. By this time, I felt so unworthy of God's forgiveness that I made a choice to abort my child, which led me further into despair, shame and regret.

After marrying again and beginning our family, I became aware that the shame for my past was haunting me all the time, which would lead me to continually ask for forgiveness yet never really feel completely forgiven.

Ten years ago, God led us to leave our Canadian home and move to California, where He began to woo me to trust Him with my past and show me that I needed healing for my past as well as forgiveness. At the time I was teaching abstinence for a pregnancy center, speaking to youth about saving sex for marriage. As I was teaching others, God began to use what I was learning about the brain and sex to show me how my past was still hurting me. Following God's leading, I first went through healing for my abortion and then went through sexual healing.

At first, I thought I was the only one who had messed up as a Christian, but when I began to share that God had broken the bonds I'd made in my past, allowing me to re-bond with my husband, I began to have lines of people asking me how they could break their bonds. That led me to write my first book, *The Invisible Bond*. Shortly after that, our pastor of women's ministry asked me to start a Bible study for sexual healing for our women. Since there was no study like this, I ended up writing my own Bible study, and after leading hundreds of women through healing, God revealed to me more specifically how sex from the past was hurting married women.

God then led me to write my second book, *Kiss Me Again*, restoring lost intimacy in marriage. It's been an amazing journey to hear from people all over the world, whom God is setting free, healing them from past and present hurts and struggles. He has redeemed my past and turned my mess into a message of healing and hope for others. I'm forever grateful to Him. I thought I was on the shelf, but God in His grace has chosen to take what the enemy meant for evil and use it in His amazing Kingdom work for good.

Carole: What about people who need healing from the breakup of a relationship?

Barbara: Science has shown that when we're in emotional pain from breakups involving sex, the chronic release of endorphins as a natural pain reliever inhibits the production and release of oxytocin. Unfortunately, having many adverse sexual experiences can completely inhibit our ability to bond in subsequent relationships. But with healing the wounds from our past, reversing the lies we've ingrained, breaking past bonds and grieving our losses because of our past, we're no longer in emotional pain, eliminating the chronic release of endorphins.

And this is how amazing God is . . . when we stop releasing endorphins chronically, we are able to produce and release oxytocin again, allowing us to bond. I see this happening every week with the women I get to lead through healing. It's so awesome!

Carole: You're frequently interviewed on radio, and you speak often to groups about this important subject of how sexual promiscuity causes what has become your mission field: wounded and bleeding souls with damaged hearts, damaged relationship and damaged marriages. Tell us about your experience at the United Nations Summit 2010, a conference on the Status of Women.

Barbara: Wow, it was so amazing! God opened doors for us to speak to influential delegates from all over the world. We spoke to the delegates from Iraq, Nigeria, Zambia, Namibia and other places. I distributed my books and materials to the delegates to take home to their countries. I've already had requests to go to some of these countries to share this message. We even had an opportunity to speak to the ambassador to the U.S. delegation in a private meeting.

One of my favorite opportunities was to meet Sarah Palin and give her two signed copies of my books, one to her and one to her daughter Bristol. I'm praying that God uses these contacts to open more doors for His message of truth and healing.

Carole: Even men and women of God are not immune to sexual temptation. I've written about the life of David, always described as a man after God's own heart. But, as you know, he also stumbled and fell into sexual sin. What do you say to Christians who have stumbled and fallen in this way?

Barbara: I spent several decades letting my messy past keep me from coming close to God. I'm not sure where I got the idea that we needed to clean ourselves up to come to God.

But as I've shared with others, I've discovered that we all sin, and that sexual sin, although not worse than other sins, is different in that it causes greater wounding, which is why God has tried to protect us with His boundaries of saving sex for marriage.

I also find that people suffering from the shame of a sexual past and the things associated with it—such as abortion, homosexuality and pornography—want to keep silent about it, hoping to deal with it on their own. The truth is, it won't go away on its own. You need to bring it to God, and allow Him to heal it and set you free from the shame and pain. It will always keep you from complete wholeness and freedom physically, spiritually and emotionally. God has His arms open to you, beckoning you to come and receive His forgiveness and healing. He just wants you to be free to enjoy your relationship with Him. He cares less about the sin of your past and more about you in the present . . . and your relationship with Him. Don't let it keep you in silent shame and bondage one more day. Let God have it, and let Him set you free completely and forever.

Carole: What's your best advice to readers of *Hope 4 You* for following God's plan for physical intimacy?

Barbara: I've discovered that Satan is our greatest enemy to sexual intimacy. Before marriage, he tries to get us to have sex. Once we're married, he tries to keep us from having sex. In both cases, it destroys us and our relationships.

God is not trying to spoil our fun or ruin our lives when He says to save sex for marriage; He wants to protect us from creating past bonds that will inhibit our marital bond and hurt intimacy in marriage. God designed sex in marriage to be the bond that brings life, intimacy and deepening, growing love. But outside of marriage that bond is destructive, bringing pain, shame, brokenness and heartache, and also leading to possible sexual addictions or dysfunctions.

I encourage you, whether you're single or married, that if you've experienced sex in your past outside of marriage, whether from abuse or your own choices, let God heal you so that you can be whole in a future or present relationship. If you're married, God can break past bonds so that you can re-bond with your spouse, or maybe have a brand-new bond. If you're single, healing will set you free from past relationships so that, as a healthy person, you'll know how to pick a healthy mate, how to build a healthy relationship and be able to bond in marriage.

For Study

1. Fill in the missing words from this chapter's Bible verse:

   But those who ________________________ in the Lord will renew their ________________. They will soar on wings like ____________; they will ________ and not grow weary, they will _____________ and not be faint (Isa. 40:31).

2. This chapter is packed with examples of ways we wait on God, who is the source of all our hope. Describe a circumstance in your life that taught you the importance of waiting on God.

   ____
   ____
   ____
   ____
   ____

3. Describe three "waiting" circumstances that need prayer, especially in the context of waiting on God. These circumstances can be in your life, in the lives of loved ones or people you know. Commit to praying for these circumstances.

   ____
   ____
   ____
   ____
   ____

Heavenly Father, You know what is best for us as Your children. Thank You for having patience, but also for prodding us to wait for You, to do that which is in our best interests as we grow into Christlike people who long to serve You every day. Amen.

12

Faith Revitalizes Hope

For God so loved the world, that he gave his one and only Son, that whoever believes in him shall not perish but have eternal life.
JOHN 3:16

We are nearing the end of *Hope 4 You*. How could I do justice to the concept of hope without talking about how faith revitalizes hope?

I believe that John 3:16 is the most hope-filled verse in the Bible. God loved you and me so much that He sent His one and only Son, Jesus, to this earth. Jesus lived among the people for only 33 years. He lived a sinless life, healed the sick, restored sight to the blind and caused the lame to walk again. He was nailed to a cross where He died, bearing the sins of the people of that day and of every person born ever since.

Three days after His death, He rose again and is now in heaven, sitting at the right hand of God, interceding for you and me. By accepting this free gift of salvation, we become children of God, and when we die, we will go to heaven to live forever. But I believe the most exciting thing about accepting Jesus into our lives is that His Holy Spirit comes to live inside us, and through His power teaches us how to live righteously in this world.

"Hopeless" is a word that describes anyone who doesn't know Jesus Christ personally. Knowing about Him is not enough. Each of us must accept Him into our heart and believe that He lived a sinless life, died for our sins and rose again after three days in the grave.

Most everyone who is a Christian has family members and friends who do not know Jesus Christ personally. Most of the time we feel helpless about it, and it doesn't seem that anything we say makes any difference in their lives. We pray for their salvation; but sometimes years go by without any change.

In the previous chapter we had a compelling interview with a woman whose husband says he has fallen away from faith, a hard concept to understand and accept. You may wonder if his faith was ever real. Only God knows the answer to that. But the painful situation of Christians who are married or related to non-believers is *very real.*

This chapter is written for those who feel hopeless that people they love will ever come to Christ and claim Him as their Savior. You might have even stopped praying for them because you now believe their situation is hopeless. My prayer for you is that the stories you read in this chapter will restore your faith in the power of God to change lives and that you will begin praying fervently again for those you love.

My Faith Walk Begins

Readers of my previous books may recall that my own faith story began when I was five years old. In the fall of 1942, when I was nine months old, my mom and dad moved from Oklahoma City, where I was born. Our country was embroiled in World War II, and my dad came to Houston because there was work at the shipyard. My sister, Glenda, was seven years older than I, and the four of us settled into life in Houston.

My parents were good people who didn't know Jesus. They played poker every Friday night with friends, and my sister and I would curl up and go to sleep on the sofa. A couple who owned a neighborhood drug store began taking my sister and me to church every week. One Sunday, when Glenda was 12 and I was 5, her choir was scheduled to sing in church. My mom was sick and stayed home, but my dad went to hear my sister sing, and he was miraculously saved that morning. He came home and told my mom what happened, and she went back to church with him that night and accepted Jesus as well.

My parents joined the church and were baptized, and our lives were all radically changed from that day forward. We went to church on Sunday morning, Sunday night and Wednesday night as well. I remember attending Sunday School parties with my parents, and my sister and I were involved in every activity the church offered. My mother used to say, "We didn't have to drop our old friends at all. They dropped us like hot potatoes when they found out what had happened to us."

I accepted Jesus as my Savior when I was 12 years old, and my life has never been the same. I have deserted Jesus many times, but He has never deserted me. He has been there since the day that I invited Him into my heart, loving me and teaching me His ways.

My nephew Rick told me that he wants to write a book entitled *The Power of One*. It would be based on the ripple effect that happens in families like mine: Because my dad went to church to hear my sister sing that Sunday morning, our entire family now knows and serves Jesus Christ. What power there is in just one person coming to faith in Christ!

More Real-life Stories

I attended a Christmas party with my daughter Lisa and heard the story you will read below. At that party, I met a young woman named Karen, who moved to Houston because her husband is working here as an engineer doing contract work with a Houston company. I was captivated by Karen from the minute we met. Her Virginia drawl, her warmth and her love for God and His Son, Jesus, were mesmerizing.

Karen married at 16, had two children before she was 19 and lost her husband to cancer after 20 years of marriage. Here she is today, living in Houston and remarried to a godly husband. They have a beautiful three-year-old girl named Ava. She has a 25-year-old daughter and a 23-year-old son in North Carolina, and God has been good to Karen and filled her heart with joy.

When Karen told me the story of her mother's salvation, I knew that I must share it with you—in her own words. May it fill you with hope for your loved ones who need Jesus in their lives.

Karen's Story of Her Mom

Mom was born March 13, 1937, in the hills of Virginia. She was the last born and the thirteenth child of a saw miller and his wife in Wolf Pin Holler. Her mother was a busy, hard-working woman. She made all the family's clothing and soap, and she tended a large garden. Most of the daily care this new baby, named Pearl, received came from my Aunt Dot, her older sister. But, by any standard, Pearl was loved and cherished by the entire family, as is often the case concerning the baby of the bunch.

She told me her father carried her to the table for breakfast every day and was still doing so when she was eight years old. That's when he was killed in an accident at work. Life for my mother was a lot harder after that, but she had a strong spirit and was always able to be thankful for what she had.

She didn't go to school until she was 12 years old, but was so very proud of the fact that she had graduated sixth grade. She was the only one in her family who could read and write, so this was a great help to all those around her.

She met my father at church when she was 18, and after a brief and well-chaperoned courtship, they were married. They set up housekeeping in a one-room shack with conditions that would horrify me, but my mother would smile and talk fondly of that time in her life.

Soon after the wedding, my father became an abusive drunk, and the moonshine flowed as freely as the bluegrass music. To be a drunk and to abuse and neglect your family must have been accepted in the area in which we lived.

My father always had a new truck and pockets full of money. He worked two shifts in the coal mines and must have been good at what he did. He just never seemed to be able to recognize the needs of his family. He was generous with all those around us, especially the single women, but it didn't seem to bother him that his wife and children cried themselves to sleep at night because their stomachs ached from being so hungry.

I don't know how my mother stood it, but she had five children and then a set of twins. I was one of those twins, and when we were two years old, our daddy and the older children went to visit an aunt who lived nearby. One day while they were gone, my mother was washing clothes on an old wringer washer on the porch. My twin sister and I were playing on a quilt close to our momma, but she was working so hard that she must have taken her eyes off of us right at the moment when we wandered out to the yard. There was an old well in the yard that wasn't deep, but my sister Sharon fell into it head first.

When my mother found us, she pulled Sharon out by her feet and ran screaming up the road to try to find help. A coal truck driver stopped, chased my mother down and tried to do CPR on Sharon, but it was too late. I don't remember any of this, but they say my mother wanted to die. She was seven months pregnant at the time, and people blamed my mother, and so did my father, for what happened to my sister.

My mother continued to care for her children and continued having children without the things a woman needs: healthcare, nutrition, the love of her husband or even support from friends and family. You see, we usually lived way back in a holler, and with no driver's license or a way to go anywhere, you can't go visiting. Besides that, people never really wanted to see such a big crowd as us standing on their door stoop.

My mother never had the luxury of a close friend, and this breaks my heart, for I never would have made it this far if God had not given me true, godly friends to help me along the way. I remember we lived on a high hill, and my brother and I would stand at the window watching my mother try to climb the steep, ice-covered slope to our house. She had a feed sack full of coal on her back, which we needed to heat the house. She would take a step or two and fall, catch herself with her ungloved hands, then get up and fall again. It was a long endeavor and painful to watch, but she never gave up.

I remember coming home from school one day, complaining that we had to take our shoes off for P.E. class to jump on the trampoline. My socks didn't match, plus they were old, stained and full of holes. The kids got a special kick out of saying I didn't know how to match my socks, because one was blue and one was brown.

When I told my mom about it, she held me tight and told me she was sorry. That evening, life went on as usual, but the next morning when I went to put my shoes on, there was a pair of matching socks! My mother had cut off her sweater sleeves to make me a pair of socks. Now, I know that most of us have a closet full of sweaters, so this might not seem like much, but my mother had one old sweater and no coat. She still wore this old sweater because it was all she had. I am still filled with sadness when I think of her thin arms going bare.

I remember that when we only had one piece of bread to share among us, which was the norm, she would say she wasn't hungry. The love she gave us and the sacrifices she made for us made up for the shame of our poverty.

When I was 12 years old, I guess my mother's spirit finally broke. The frequent beatings, the hunger and the loneliness eventually took their toll on her, because, you see, she didn't know the Lord. She became an alcoholic—a mirror to my father—and just as bad as he was. She used to say, "If you can't beat 'em, join 'em."

After that, it was like she just handed me all her responsibilities and the rearing of my four younger siblings. I was so angry with life and the loss of my mother. Her body was still around, but it now held a mean, hateful drunk who had to be cared for, as well as the children.

By the grace of God, we children survived. When I was 23 years old, I got a call saying my father was being airlifted to the closest trauma center, because he had shot himself in the head. I asked where my mom was, and they said she was still at the house. When I got there, I found her sitting in a drunken stupor with blood all over her, wondering what had happened. After I bathed and dressed her, we went to the hospital, and we never left his side. He died three days later, and my mother was so helpless she couldn't even bathe herself. I did what I had to do to help her get through the funeral, but without my knowing it, my husband told her she could come live with us.

I was so angry, because I didn't even *like* this woman anymore. After 12 years as an alcoholic, she had become a really awful person, and I couldn't believe I would now have to live with her in my house. Well, the rule in our family was, if you lived in our house, you had to go to church. So my mother went with us to church, even though later she would still go off with others and come home drunk. She would hide beer in the house, which would make me furious, but she kept going to church with us.

About two months after the death of my father, my mother gave her heart to Jesus, and the immediate transformation had to be seen to be believed. Before she got saved, her mouth was so vile; but after she got saved, she never said a bad word about anybody. The fact that her language was cleaned up was a miracle—before that, she'd never been able to talk without cussing.

My mother became so filled with the love of Jesus that she was a pleasure to be around, and she was loved by anyone fortunate enough to know her. She left this world 10 years later after a bout with cancer. In her last hours, in her unconscious state, with all her children around her bed singing her favorite hymns, we saw an amazing sight. Her eyes opened and she looked upward, and a smile appeared on her tired, thin face. She kept this expression until the end, and we are all convinced she saw wonderful things we were not able to see.

God gave us back our mother even though the devil tried to destroy her. We never doubt where she is, and I look forward to the day when I can tell her again how much I love her.

I have a dear friend, Margaret Lloyd, who has committed to pray for me every day. She has a copy of my calendar, and we try to meet on a regular basis to pray together and to catch up on each other's lives. Last month, when we met together, she shared a story with me that is sure to bring hope to you as well. This is the story of Kathy Johnson's father. Kathy is a member of our church. She was kind enough to write her story for me, and what a story it is!

Kathy Johnson's Story

My God performed a miracle on September 30, 2009! My father, Jack Maurice Burden, accepted Jesus Christ as his Lord and Savior.

Throughout my life, I was never sure of my father's salvation. He believed in God and that Jesus was the Son of God, but he would never commit to the belief that one man could take away the sins of the world. My dad was a great man, a wonderful father and a faithful husband. He was a loving man, and I would call him a gentleman, but he would not talk to me about Jesus.

I began praying for my father's salvation around 1978, after I began studying God's Word.

I asked several friends and my Sunday School class to keep him in their prayers. I was faithful to pray at times, but not fervently, as I should have.

In 2002, my father was diagnosed with Alzheimer's. I became more vigilant about my prayers, asking God to give me windows of opportunity to speak to my dad about

Christ and His wonderful gift of salvation. I asked my sister if she remembered the night in our living room, years ago, when I thought Dad said yes to the minister. She did not remember.

On September 25, 2008, we had to place Dad in an Alzheimer's unit in an assisted living facility. All hope seemed gone. I grieved over the fact that his mind had deteriorated and he was not communicating much anymore.

On September 15 of the following year, almost a year to the day after his arrival in the Alzheimer's unit, his caregiver called to say Dad was not eating, not drinking and was not responsive. I stayed with him every day for two weeks and three days, praying over him, singing hymns and reading Scripture, begging God to open his mind, begging God to save my father. I felt that God had forsaken me, and I cried and pleaded with Him like never before.

On September 24, my dear friend Margaret Lloyd called me to ask a random question, not knowing that my father was so close to death. When I told her his condition, she responded with that great cliché: "Well, at least he's going to heaven." I lost it—"No," I blurted out, "we don't know if he's going to heaven." Margaret felt so bad! She apologized and added that now she remembered we'd prayed for his salvation before. Naturally, feeling awful, she immediately began storming heaven's gate for God to wake up my dad just long enough to hear the gospel from some human being or from Jesus Himself!

On the morning of September 29, during my quiet time, I read from my Oswald Chambers devotional. It was all about God using supernatural ways—inexpressible ways. My heart began to fill with great hope and joy. Then my devotional by Chris Tiegreen talked about needing companions to help—two are better than one, but three are the best (see Eccles. 4:8-12). I didn't think about my friends while reading the devotional; I focused more on the fact that God is capable of working any kind of miracle.

Wednesday, September 30, while kneeling beside Dad's bed, I began to pray over him with such power and conviction. I began telling him this was the end, and he could only be in heaven through the death and resurrection of Jesus Christ. He was listening, but his face was frightened. He was looking all around the room through wide, scared eyes.

I received a text message from my dear friend Beverly Newman, saying she was praying for me for strength with God's power—praying Colossians 1:11 at that very moment! It gave me boldness, so I continued trying to reach Dad. When I presented the gospel, asking Dad if he could believe in his heart that Jesus died for his sins, and accept His free gift of salvation, he said in a loud angry voice: "No!" His face looked so frightened. I strongly told him, "This is it—your last chance." I told him he was experiencing spiritual warfare—that demons were trying to take him straight to hell! I explained that God had kept his heart beating these last two weeks because God was fighting for him; yet Satan and his demons were trying to keep him away from the truth.

At that moment, I received another text message from my friend Susan Newman (who isn't related to my other friend with the same last name). Susan was praying for me to be strong. So I continued with renewed strength, presenting the gospel again, telling my daddy that God loved him *so* much, that He had created him 87 years ago and did not want to lose him. I told Dad his death did not have to be a scary time and that, if he would choose Christ, God would send His angels and he would have peace. I asked him again, "Can you believe in your heart that Jesus Christ died for your sins so that you can have His righteousness to stand before God and live forever and ever with God in heaven? Do you understand? Can you believe in your heart that Jesus is the only way?"

At that moment, Dad's face began to soften, and he smiled and whispered, "Yes, I can!"

I praised God! He kept smiling, and his eyes turned crystal clear as he became alert and woke up to the truth. He looked like my dad again. He began licking his lips, so I asked him if he was thirsty, and he said yes. I ran to the kitchen, yelling, "My dad's awake—he accepted Jesus as his Savior!" One of the caregivers yelled back, "I knew there were demons in that room!"

We gave him water, and he drank half a glass without any problem, which was a miracle in itself (he had not been able to swallow for two weeks prior to that without choking). I asked if he was hungry, and he said clearly, "A little bit." He ate half a cup of vanilla pudding. He sat up, looking totally normal, and laughing and talking to two workers who came into his room. He looked across the room and noticed something we'd had there since he moved in—a model airplane and an American flag (he was a retired lieutenant colonel in the Texas Air National Guard). With a clear voice and sparkling eyes, he asked, "Is that an airplane next to that flag?"

For 30 minutes my dad came back to life! He had peace and joy.

While all this was happening, my sister-in-law called, but I told her I had to call her back. Finally, I called my sister and mother and told them Dad had awakened and accepted Christ and that he was drinking, eating, laughing and talking. I told them to come quickly.

He started to close his eyes and went back to sleep. I called my sister-in-law back to tell her the great news, and she asked me when this all happened. When I told her it was between 8:00 and 8:30, she said that was the exact time she was praying, asking God to give me a miracle! She was the third strand of the cord "not quickly broken" that I had read about in Ecclesiastes 4:12.

Dad went to be with the Lord at 9:00 P.M. on October 2, 2009—two days after receiving Christ as his Savior. Praise be to God!

Martha Marks is a precious lady in my First Place 4 Health class. Ever since she joined our class she has been able to say all 10 of our Scripture memory verses on the last day of class at our Victory Celebration. God's Word is very important to Martha, and she is committed to memorizing it faithfully. The first two real-life stories in this chapter were about parents who came to know Christ; but this one is about how Martha came to accept Jesus personally into her life after being raised in an Orthodox Jewish home. She calls her story of hope "Miracles from Ashes."

Martha Marks's Story

As I write this, I am filled with amazement at the Lord's ability to bring resurrection from ashes. My spiritual journey toward faith in Christ has been an immense struggle, but God has triumphed against all odds. It is my hope that my story will encourage others to press on and never assume that the doorway to Christ is closed to them.

I was raised by incredibly loving parents and brought up in the Jewish faith. My precious father is a survivor of the Nazi Holocaust and the most courageous person I have ever known. In 1944, at the age of 14, he was deported with his parents from Budapest, Hungary, to the Auschwitz concentration camp. His beloved parents would be murdered upon arrival there. He would be sent to three other death camps, where he endured and witnessed unspeakable atrocities.

After the war ended, my dad immigrated to Houston, Texas, where he met my mom. They married and had three children. Our little family was tightly knit, because we understood the fragility of life. We absolutely cherished one another.

Dad worked as a musician, and music was a life-sustaining comfort to him. When I was seven, he brought home a tiny, half-size violin for me to try. I instantly fell in love with it, and it became my second voice. Through the strings, I could cry out the pain I felt over the fate of the Hungarian Jews—pain that words could never express. In childhood photos, I am rarely seen without my violin.

When I was nine, Mom was diagnosed with breast cancer. One late night, Dad came home from the hospital and cried at the kitchen table. He had no idea I was awake and watching him. Since he was always optimistic and cheerful (survival techniques he clung to), I knew something was very wrong. That night I made a decision to do the unthinkable—to pray to Jesus. Secretly, I climbed into bed and begged Jesus not to take anyone from my father. Mom recovered completely after surgery, and I never took her life for granted. This experience sparked my first mustard seed of faith in the Jesus I knew nothing about.

I celebrated my Bat Mitzvah at age 13 and enjoyed learning all of the Old Testament—especially the psalms. Still, I craved more. Becoming a professional violinist in my late teens, I often performed in churches. Sermons would touch my heart, but other than politely bowing my head, I did not allow myself to pray publicly in a church. A persistent sense of grief and loss engulfed me, but I chose to cover it up with layers of music, plus a comedic and extroverted personality and compulsive overeating.

When thoughts of Jesus popped up, I dismissed them immediately. I was lucky enough to live in America and be free from persecution. Conversion out of our faith could *not* happen for me. Millions had paid with their lives—the ultimate price—and I was proud of my parents and my Jewish heritage. Breaking my father's heart was out of the question. Jesus would just have to stop tugging at my soul, because I could never answer His call. How little comprehension of God's power I had.

Feeling trapped, I discovered that food made me feel better. I began to eat constantly and lived for the comfort of every meal. In my twenties, I began performing with symphony orchestras around the world. On the road, the exciting foreign places allowed me to escape from reality for a while.

My sweet, younger brother is autistic and mentally disabled. His daily battles to function and access badly needed care were traumatic. Both my parents lavished him with love through difficult days. The stress continued to snowball when my older sister was diagnosed with late-stage aggressive breast cancer in 1992. Her prognosis was dismal. The old childhood fear of death and loss again reared its ugly head. My overriding thought was, "Oh, no, my poor father. She absolutely *cannot die!*"

Working in the Dallas Opera Orchestra, I begged Christian friends to pray for her. They started massive chains of 24-hour prayer coverage. I moved back to Houston to care for her and gave up the job I loved. After surgery, chemo and radiation treatment, my sister went into remission. Now, 17 years later, she remains cancer free. Defying earthly logic, she had beaten the odds. I was now thinking seriously about the Jesus people I had turned to in the darkest times. Miracles were piling up.

God finally put an end to my running away from Him in 1997. While playing in the national tour of a Broadway show, I suffered a career-ending neck injury. My escape vehicle—the violin—was gone. I would never play again. I returned home to Houston permanently, a caged bird with clipped wings.

During that time, concerned musician friends took me to church with them. The kindness of people there lifted my spirits. After two years of Bible study with them, I knew I must follow my heart. I could not live another day without the comforting words of Jesus and the fellowship of believers.

Miserable with shame, inner conflict and guilt, I told my parents that I wanted to be baptized and join a church.

My adorable father said, "I know what it is to lose a family. Don't worry. I am not going to lose you over this." Mom selflessly tried to support me, hiding whatever pain she felt.

On the day of my baptism, I spoke at all four worship services in my large church. Returning home alone and exhausted emotionally, I found a jewelry box by the front door of my tiny apartment. Opening it, I discovered a beautiful silver necklace with a cross on it. It was a gift from my remarkable parents. I was overcome with a mixture of joy and gratitude. Our miracle-working God had filled us all with the grace to love each other through this transition in my life.

Today, I share my testimony as a Christian speaker and comedienne. I met Carole Lewis in 2008, when we both spoke at a women's conference. This encounter was a Divine appointment. I weighed 230 pounds on a five-foot frame and had chest pains and morbid obesity. Carole offered to help me through First Place 4 Health. I knew that Jesus had sent an angel to save my life.

With total commitment, I threw myself into the program. I am thrilled to have lost 40 pounds and many inches and dress sizes. This is only the beginning, because I intend to press on. And with the Lord's help, I will lose 50 more pounds and reach my goal this year.

My brother now receives excellent care in a loving community for the mentally disabled. The message I proclaim is one of hope despite earthly circumstances. With God all things are possible. Never ever give up. As my favorite Scripture teaches, "Blessed are those who mourn, for they will be comforted" (Matt. 5:4).

Here is one last interview on the subject of reaching out in faith, which can be overwhelming. Do we really believe that God will give us the nudge and the tools? Or do we think the entire burden is on us to become motivated, to "get up and go"? Listen in on this section of an interview I did with a friend named Megan.

Interview with Megan Heath

Carole: Megan, you say you've had a problem with trust. That's a common problem, even among some believers. Can we really lay our needs at the feet of Jesus?

Megan: Yes, the issue is really this: Does God care about the little things in life that mean a lot to us? Sometimes we feel silly approaching Him with day-to-day issues. After all, He is the God of the entire universe!

Carole: So tell us what this has to do with your alarm clock?

Megan: Oh, yeah, the Lord started waking me up. I made a commitment to rise early so I could spend time alone with Him at the beginning of the day. Well, very soon into the process I found that no matter how early I set my alarm, He would wake me up about two minutes before it was due to go off.

Carole: What do you think this meant?

Megan: I think God was showing me that I could *try* to be in control by setting my alarm clock, but He would be the one to wake me up.

Carole: So this was confirmation that He cared about your goals.

Megan: It was also confirmation that I do not have to lean on my own efforts. He is with me every step of the way.

Carole: How long has this been going on?

Megan: In November it will be two years.

Carole: Let's not miss the point that you are deliberately and intentionally walking with Him. You are making an effort, and—because He knows your heart—He sees your faithfulness.

Megan: Yes . . .

Carole: This would be a different outcome if you were just doing your own thing and then trusting Him to wake you up. "Oh, Lord, I feel like staying up until 3:00, but will You wake me up at 5:00 anyway?"

Megan: Exactly.

For Study

1. Does someone you love need Jesus? If so, your job is to pray. God's job is to orchestrate the circumstances of his or her life so that person has every opportunity to come to know Him. Releasing our loved ones to God and His perfect will and plan for their lives is the first step in restoring our faith that God can and will bring our loved ones to Christ.

   List the people you know have prayed for you, or you suspect have prayed for you, your salvation and your growth as a follower of Christ.

2. List people you know who need Jesus in their life. Place a checkmark beside the names of those you will commit to add to your prayer list.

3. Write a prayer telling God that you are willing to release these people so that He can do whatever it takes to bring them to faith in Him. Ask God to use you for His purposes in this mission.

____

____

____

____

____

____

____

Thank You, Lord, for selecting our families just for us. Sometimes we don't know why You chose those particular family members for us, but we recognize that Your purposes are perfect, because You are the perfect Father. Amen.

13

There Is Hope 4 You

For in this hope we were saved. But hope that is seen is no hope at all.
Who hopes for what he already has?
But if we hope for what we do not yet have, we wait for it patiently.
ROMANS 8:24-25

I saw an advertisement that began with a question: "Are you mature enough . . ." and then it went on to list items from the past such as black and white television, cassette tapes and car telephones.

The idea gave me a good laugh. I knew exactly what the ad copywriters were doing, and I approved wholeheartedly. Instead of asking if their readers were *old* enough, they asked if they were *mature* enough. The implication is that with age comes maturity and with maturity comes wisdom.

First Place 4 Health has participants and leaders of every age. However, I've noticed a certain maturity about them that defies their chronological age. They have these attitudes in common:

- Each one has made a deliberate and intentional decision to improve their health.
- Each one defines health in these four areas: physical, mental, emotional, spiritual.
- Each one recognizes God's desire for them to experience balance in all four areas.
- Each one has accepted full responsibility for improving their personal health.
- Each one has a plan—as well as a promise to God—for improving their health.

These are people who are striving to know God's plan and purposes for their life and to seek those first every day.

They have discovered a thing or two (or three) about health. Yes, it involves planning how to eat and how to exercise—and then carrying through with those plans—but it also involves other elements of life:

- Good health means enjoying a good belly laugh every day.
- Good health means giving yourself a pat on the back for accomplishments.
- Good health means seeking out people who share your faith commitment.
- Good health means hiding God's Word in your heart.
- Good health means sharing your faith (and health) journey with others.

The list could go on and on, of course. I strongly encourage you to add your own. Marilyn Bullock is a First Place 4 Health member who personifies the attitude that leads to success. I took a nice walk with her one year at Wellness Week. She said she had lost 60 pounds by her fiftieth birthday. Although she occasionally gains some of it back, she returns to the process of putting God first and loses it again. She has even decided to invest in the health of two other people by inviting them to join the program and come to Wellness Week. Now that's love and friendship! It's also a great example of the commitment to share your faith (and health) journey with others.

More Real-life Stories

These first-person stories will amaze, motivate and bless you.

The people you've met throughout this book are concerned with their health. They have grown through the variety of life experiences they've shared through their stories, and they incorporate healthful principles into their daily living. Many are involved in the First Place 4 Health program.

A fun part of my role as national director of First Place 4 Health is to meet participants and hear their stories. I always include several in my books. This chapter is dedicated to those people in the program, a few of whom you will meet here.

They represent only a smattering of our success stories. You'll find others on our website. God bless the people who were willing to add their wit and wisdom to *Hope 4 You*. And God bless you for reading the book and learning that there is hope for you too.

Becoming a First Place 4 Health Leader

By Michelle Cresap

My "before" picture was taken on November 8, 2006, the day I received the Mississippi School Counselor of the Year award. This should have been one of the happiest days of my life; unfortunately, it was not. Numerous health issues made it almost impossible for me even to attend the ceremony.

Later, I had several surgeries, and the doctor diagnosed me with diabetes. I was placed on four insulin shots a day. I was at my heaviest—250 pounds. I knew I had to do something or I was going to die.

I read a book by Carole Lewis about First Place 4 Health and decided to try the program. With limited biblical knowledge, I felt hesitant to lead a group. Initially, I did part of the steps of First Place 4 Health on my own. Then the Lord revealed to me that through Him I could lead a group.

I bought a leadership kit; and in April 2008, we started First Place 4 Health at Hickory Ridge Baptist Church in Florence, Mississippi. This marked the beginning of a journey that would forever change my life.

A couple of months later, the program was revised. In my discouragement I searched the First Place 4 Health website where I found Joyce Ainsworth, a leader at a nearby church. She inspired me to continue with the new and improved program. Joyce is now the networking leader for Mississippi and continues to be my mentor.

I have lost 84 pounds, and my health has improved drastically. I no longer have to take insulin or any form of diabetes medicine. My diabetes is controlled through the new lifestyle Jesus has shown me and has enabled me to live.

More important, I have gained so much more than I have lost. I now have a personal relationship with Jesus that grows stronger each day. I know more Bible verses than I ever learned as a kid. I have bonded with a group of ladies I can call on at any time. I can even play tag with my little boy!

I have always struggled with my weight. But when I finally let Jesus be Lord of my life and not just my Savior, I have been able to balance my life mentally, physically, emotionally and spiritually. The first memory verse I learned in First Place 4 Health says it all:

> But seek first his kingdom and his righteousness, and all these things will be given to you as well (Matt. 6:33).

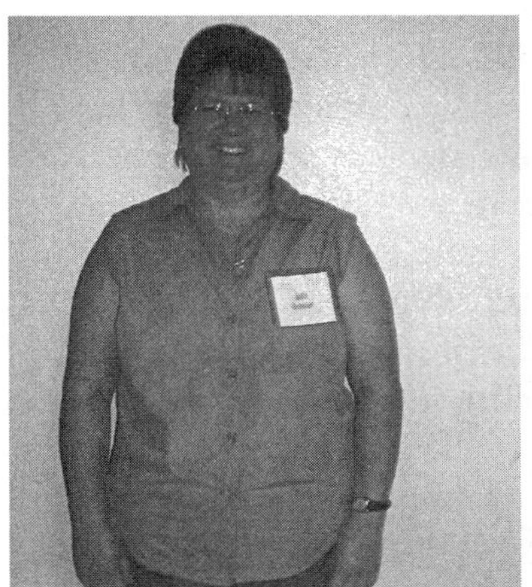

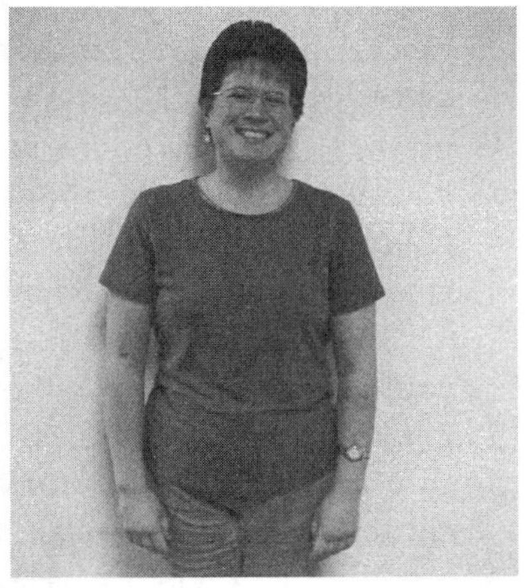

Putting God First

By Julie Schuler

I had never really given God first place in my life. He always came up last. My issues with putting God last in my life included not understanding His Word and being overweight. I had been praying to God for quite some time that He would send someone to help me with my struggle to understand the Bible. I never felt like He heard me.

I received an email from a friend one day about this program called First Place 4 Health. I decided to attend the orientation, not knowing what I was getting myself into.

On the night of the orientation, I walked into a church I had never heard of before, where I only knew one person, the leader of the class. Listening to all the information that night was so overwhelming. I reluctantly signed up for First Place 4 Health. I knew I was way out of my comfort zone. However, the more I thought about it, the more I started putting this "out of my comfort zone" feeling into a different light.

I told myself for the first time that it's not about me; this is for God. Once classes started and we got into the Bible study, I was really struggling. I could do the food part of the program with no problem. I was losing weight easily. But the Bible study was a different story. By week seven, we were asked to write a testimony of something great that God had done in our life. That was it for me. I had to tell my leader that there was nothing great that God had done in my life. I didn't even understand "His Word," the Bible. I called myself a "struggling Christian."

I met my class leader at her house one night so she could help me with the Bible study. Well, we never even got around to the studies. We talked about my relationship with God, salvation and all my past experiences with churches. God knew all along what He was doing when I received that first email. He had heard my prayers all this time about sending someone to help me in my struggle with His Word. He answered my prayer in His time, not mine. I rededicated my life to Christ that night and was filled with the Holy Spirit. It was the most amazing thing.

My life has not been the same since. I can feel God all around me and see what He is doing in my life. I understand the Bible for the first time. Since starting First Place 4 Health in September 2007, I have lost 57 pounds. I went from 177 pounds down to 120 pounds. I was wearing size 20 pants and now wear a size 6/8. My blood pressure has come down, and I have been able to go off one of my blood pressure pills. I might be able to go off the other blood pressure pill in a few months. My cholesterol and sugar levels also have come down significantly. But most important, God is now first in my life where He belongs. I know that nothing is possible without Him. He has truly blessed me.

He reached down from on high and took hold of me;
he drew me out of deep waters.
2 SAMUEL 22:17

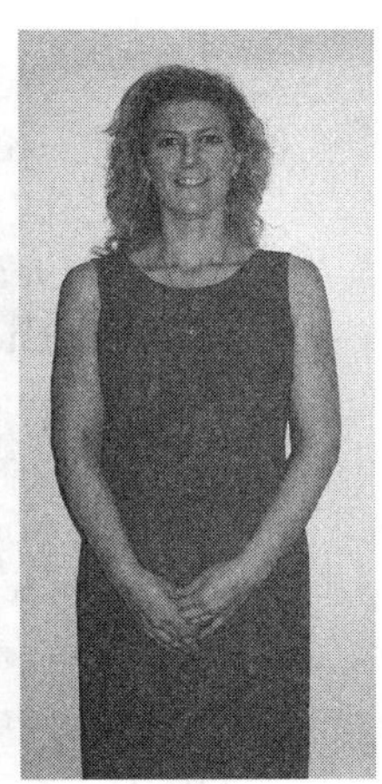

Putting God First Changed My Life

By Rachel Dennis

I am so blessed that First Place 4 Health entered my life. It has truly changed me forever.

Here is where my journey began: Before going on vacation last year, I sat through the presentation on the four-sided person. I was reminded by my leader that I was the last person to sign up that day. Although I was at the very end of my rope from being overweight, I had tried everything else and it didn't work. So what did I have to lose, but weight! I gave the First Place 4 Health program a shot but with plenty of skepticism.

My weight problem started at around age seven. By the age of 10, I weighed 120 pounds. From that point on, I continued to gain weight by leaps and bounds. I graduated high school weighing 190 pounds. During this time, I had tried all types of diets, even to the point of being anorexic.

Shortly after graduating high school, I met my husband. The day I got married I weighed 238 pounds. After the birth of my second child, I was unable to lose all the weight. As my son approached the six-month mark, I was teetering around 250 pounds. At that point, I just accepted that I was forever going to be overweight. I felt I had to accept it or have bariatric surgery.

The day I decided to go to my first meeting changed my life forever, though I did not know it at the time. I had completed the Bible study, memorized my Scripture and started immediately to change my calorie intake. By the end of the first week, we weighed in and I was shocked. I had lost 6 pounds already. *Wow!* I thought. *How did that happen? It was too easy.*

As weeks passed, we went deeper and deeper into Bible study and Scripture. I was astounded. The pounds began to melt off just by following what the Lord had put before me. Now I have to admit that, even though the weight was coming off, I didn't begin to exercise until I was told I needed to start. So whatever the program told me to do, I obediently followed.

I pushed through the pain of fibromyalgia and the nights of being too tired to move. At the end of 12 weeks, God had performed a miracle in my life. He had given me a weight loss total of 42 pounds in 12 weeks. I was shocked. How was that possible? As I looked at that first 12 weeks, I thought to myself, *This is the first time in your life that you have prayed to God to take your weight away.* What a wonderful gift; but I wasn't done. I agreed to a year. What was God going to allow me to do through First Place 4 Health?

On March 5, 2010, I turned 30. My goal was to be 100 pounds down by that day, God willing. After I woke up that Friday morning, I stepped on the scale. I received the best present I have ever gotten. I weighed 139.4 pounds. God blessed me! All the hard work that I had put into being obedient and praying was well worth the sweat and tears.

As of this date, I have lost 111 pounds in a total of nine months, just by giving Christ control of my life. I tell people of my miracle and they ask if I have had "the surgery." I proudly say, "No! God did it—let me tell you how!"

When I get discouraged, I fall back on the principles of those very first 12 weeks—God-centered weight loss! I recall Scripture and pull from the Lord's awesome strength to get me through the challenging times. God has healed me physically, emotionally and spiritually this year. He is awesome in His might and power.

Thank you, First Place 4 Health, for saving my life and the life of my family.

For Study

1. Fill in the words from this chapter's Bible verses:

   For in this ________________________ we were saved. But hope that is seen is ________________ hope at all. Who hopes for what he already has? But if we hope for what we ___ ______ _______ _________, we wait for it patiently (Rom. 8:24-25).

2. Write a list of three new insights or ideas you have gained from this book that you can apply to your life immediately.

   ____

   ____

   ____

   ____

   ____

   ____

   ____

   ____

3. Draw the arrow on your hope meter one more time, showing how it has changed since the last time you drew it in this book. Jot yourself notes about why you think it has changed.

Thank You, God, for giving me hope that I can change in areas of my life that will make me better able to serve You with all of myself. Please give me the courage to make these changes, knowing without a doubt that You will be with me every step of the way. Amen.

ENDNOTES

Chapter 2: Building a Fortress Around Hope

1. I am grateful to Keith W. Ward, whose article, "A Hymn of Grace: The Solid Rock" in the Spring 1998 issue of *Journal of the Grace Evangelical Society*, provided helpful information on the author of this hymn, Edward Mote (1797-1874). Mote was an English cabinetmaker for 37 years and eventually became pastor of a Baptist church in Horsham, Sussex. The son of pub owners, young Edward was often neglected by his busy parents, and he spent most of his Sundays playing in the city streets. According to Ward, "Of his theological upbringing, he said 'So ignorant was I that I did not know that there was a God.' " When he became exposed to the Word of God, he was baptized. I am fascinated that this cabinetmaker-turned-preacher also wrote hymns, including this one, which is so relevant to the concept of "building a fortress around our hope."
2. Rick Warren, quoted in Paul Bradshaw, "Living with Purpose," *Health—Bio Ethics*, August 12, 2006.
3. Ibid.
4. Ibid.
5. Mitchell's story is adapted from Bob Reccord's excellent book on building a fortress around your marriage, *Beneath the Surface: Steering Clear of the Dangers That Could Leave You Shipwrecked* (Nashville, TN: B&H Publishers, 2001).

Chapter 3: Walking with God

1. My thanks to Joyce Ainsworth for this contribution and others of hers that I used in my book *Give God a Year, Change Your Life Forever* (Ventura, CA: Regal, 2009), pp. 147-149.

Chapter 4: Praise Renews Hope

1. Jaye Martin and Terri Stovall, *Women Leading Women: The Biblical Model for the Church* (Nashville, TN: B&H Publishing Group, 2008), pp. 139-141.

Chapter 5: Prayer Revives Hope

1. Madeleine L'Engle, *Walking on Water* (Colorado Springs, CO: WaterBrook Press, 2001), p. 60.

Chapter 6: Forgiveness Restores Hope

1. Carole Lewis and Cara Symank, *The Mother-Daughter Legacy: How a Mother's Love Shapes a Daughter's Life* (Ventura, CA: Regal Books, 2004), p. 13.
2. Ibid, p. 132.

Chapter 7: Thankfulness Rekindles Hope

1. For a more complete list of circumstances for which the Holy Spirit reminded me to be thankful around the time of my daughter's death, you may be interested in my book *A Thankful Heart* (Ventura, CA: Gospel Light, 2005).
2. Additional journal pages chronicling the time before and after Hurricane Ike appear in my book *Give God a Year, Change Your Life Forever* (Ventura, CA: Gospel Light, 2009), pp. 123-135.
3. Evelyn Christenson, *Lord, Change Me!* (Colorado Springs, CO: Victor Books, Chariot/Victor Publishing, a division of Cook Communications, now David C. Cook, 1993).

Chapter 9: God's People Provide Hope

1. Virelle Kidder, *The Best Life Ain't Easy, But It's Worth It* (Chicago, IL: Moody Publishers, 2008), p. 130.

About the Author and Collaborative Author

Carole Lewis is the national director of First Place 4 Health, a Christ-centered healthy living program. A member of the original First Place group that began in 1981, she has seen the program grow from 12 groups in one church to thousands of members at more than 12,000 churches throughout the nation and in many foreign countries.

When Carole attended the First Place orientation in March 1981, she was unsure of where God was leading, but knew that she needed to make some lifestyle changes. A chance meeting with a friend from her past gave Carole the impetus to determine that she did not want to be "fat and 40." She joined a First Place group and soon lost 20 pounds. Learning how to bring balance to her life motivated her to become a First Place leader and encourage others to achieve their goals.

Carole became the national director of First Place in 1987 and is now a popular speaker and author of 12 books. Carole leads conferences, Christian spas, workshops and seminars with an emphasis on personal and spiritual balance, fitness, encouragement and temperament analysis. Her audiences know her as warm, transparent, honest and humorous.

Carole and her husband, Johnny, have three children (one deceased), eight grandchildren and two great grandchildren. They live in Houston, Texas. The books that she has written include *First Place, Choosing to Change, Today Is the First Day, Back on Track, The Mother-Daughter Legacy, The Divine Diet, A Thankful Heart, Stop It! Living Well, First Place 4 Health* and *Give God A Year.*

Carolyn Curtis is an author, editor and speaker. She has written six books and collaborated on many others. The founding editor of *On Mission* magazine, she is an award-winning writer. She has been in communication management for several corporations. She holds a Master of Arts degree in communication from Stephen F. Austin State University and a Bachelor of Journalism degree from the University of Texas at Austin. She lives in Fort Worth, Texas.

Will You Give God a Year and See What He Can Do in Your Life?

God is inviting you to go on a journey with Him. Though it may not be easy, it will be exciting!

CAROLE LEWIS is the national director of First Place 4 Health, the nation's leading Christian weight-loss program. A warm, transparent and humorous communicator, Carole is a popular speaker at conferences, fitness weeks and workshops. She and her husband, Johnny, are the proud parents of three children (one deceased) and eight grandchildren. They live in the Galveston Bay area of Texas.

Give God a Year
978.08307.51327 • $17.99

"If today you decide to give God a year by giving Christ first place every day I promise you won't be sorry!" —Carole Lewis

Order Now at Your Favorite Christian Bookseller

Experience a First Place 4 Health Miracle

Teaching New Members Is Easy!

The First Place 4 Health Kit contains everything members need to live healthy, lose weight, make friends, and experience spiritual growth. With each resource, members will make positive changes in their thoughts and emotions, while transforming the way they fuel and recharge their bodies and relate to God.

97808307.45890
$99.99 (A $145 Value!)

Member's Kit Contains:

- First Place 4 Health Hardcover Book
- Emotions & Eating DVD
- First Place 4 Health Member's Guide
- First Place 4 Health Prayer Journal
- Simple Ideas for Healthy Living
- First Place 4 Health Tote Bag
- Food on the Go Pocket Guide
- Why Should a Christian Be Physically Fit? DVD

I lost 74 pounds in 9 months!

Abby Meloy,
New Life Christian Fellowship
Lake City, Florida

I am thankful for the First Place program. As a pastor's wife who remained at the 200-pound (+) mark for seven years, I can now say I am 135 pounds, a size 8, and I have maintained this weight.

In the beginning, I did not want to try First Place 4 Health. I did not want to weigh my food or take the time to learn the measurements, but the ladies in my church wanted the program, and I was a size 18/20, so I gave it a shot. After our first session, I was 27 pounds lighter and had new insights that my body is the temple of the Holy Spirit. It took me 9 months and 3 sessions to lose 74 pounds.

My new lifestyle has influenced my husband to lose 20 pounds and my 13-year-old daughter to lose 35 pounds. We are able to carry out the work of the ministry with much less fatigue. I now teach others in my church the First Place program and will be forever grateful that the Lord brought it into my life.